Beneath The Broken Sky

Lucy Bear

Copyright © 2025 by Lucy Bear
All rights reserved. No part of this book may be reproduced in any manner whatsoever without written permission except in the case of brief quotations embodied in critical articles and reviews.
First Printing, 2025

ISBN 978-1-7386191-2-2
Softcover – Beneath the Broken Sky

Places, names, characters and events are fictitious, and any resemblance to actual persons, living or dead, or actual events is entirely coincidental.

GB PUBLISHING

Beneath The Broken Sky

About the Author

My name is Lucy Bare and I write under the pen name Lucy Bear.

In the delicate interplay between honesty and empathy, I find my voice as a storyteller. In the quiet corners of my soul, I find comfort in the embrace of the natural world and the intricate interplay of human emotions. With each stroke of my pen, I embark on a sacred journey, delving into the depths of the human spirit and the profound connections that bind us to the earth and to one another.

Through the art of words, I breathe life into characters, weaving their tales with threads of resilience, love, and the enduring strength that resides within us all. My tales transcend mere storytelling; they unfold as profound journeys of self-discovery and healing, inviting readers to navigate the intricate pathways of the heart and soul.

In the sanctuary of my stories, characters come alive, their vivid presence mirroring the complexity of human emotions. With each word, I invite readers to walk beside these characters, to feel the pulse of their challenges, savor the sweetness of their triumphs, and witness the transformative power of their journeys. It is through this intimate connection that I hope to inspire, to touch the hearts and souls of those who venture into the worlds I create.

For more about me, please visit my website:
https://www.lucybare.com/about

ALSO BY LUCY BEAR

A Winding Road to the Heart

How to Become Your Own Doula: Pocket Guide to Your Pregnancy

In Pursuit of Your Magic – A Wellness Workbook

Between the Earth and the Stars

GB PUBLISHING

CONTENTS

ABOUT THE AUTHOR iv
ALSO BY LUCY BEAR v
DEDICATION viii

1. Khalil's Desert Haven 1
2. A Love Wrapped in Twilight 5
3. Love and Conflict 13
4. Beyond Borders: Hope, love, Dreams 21
5. In The Shadow of Uncertainty 30
6. The Sisters Sanctuary 38
7. The Hearts Compass 46
8. A Nurturing Heart 50
9. Shadows and Sunshine 56
10. Love in the Distances 68
11. Between Fragments and Silence 74
12. Beneath The Rising Sun 80
13. Beneath the City's Shadows 86
14. Love Across Distances 92
15. Togetherness Dawns 102
16. Soulful Connections 112

ALSO BY LUCY BEAR   — | VII |

17 | Rising From The Ashes 125

18 | Homeward Bound 131

19 | A Distant Light 141

20 | Homecoming 154

DEDICATION

Love and Hope in a Restless World
For CMC

Dawn has always been a quiet teacher, painting the world in soft light and reminding us of the beauty in stillness. There's magic in these everyday wonders—the way sunlight filters through the trees, the scent of earth after rain, the sound of laughter shared with friends, or the warmth of a simple touch. These fleeting moments shape the essence of our lives, gently showing us the wonder in simply being alive.

I often find comfort in the stars, those quiet, shining companions in the night sky. They remind me that even in the darkest moments, we are never truly alone. There's always a light from somewhere, always within reach. Sometimes, I imagine the stars as doors to another world—an unknown space filled with things we can't quite name but feel drawn to search for. Life has a way of knowing its path. I only wish it were easier to step aside and let it unfold as it must.

The truth is life is raw and unfiltered. It doesn't wait for our hearts to heal, our minds to clear, or our spirits to steady. It moves forward—unyielding, unapologetic—nudging us to move with it. Nature teaches us how to live fully. Nature never instructs the mountains, trees, or animals on how to be; they simply exist in their true, beautiful forms. The mountains stand tall, unwavering and majestic, without anyone to tell them where to rise. Trees stretch their branches to the sky, instinctively knowing how to thrive. Animals roam the earth, reflecting freedom and resilience, without ever being told how to find their paths. They show us that there's profound beauty in living as we are, without trying to be anything else. Like them, we too can find peace by simply being ourselves.

For so long, I believed life needed to be understood—that there was some hidden logic, a grand design waiting to be uncovered. But now, I see it differently. Life isn't a puzzle to solve or a plan to uncover. There's no single purpose to chase or checklist to tick off. Life is made of fleeting moments—moments to breathe, to love, to show kindness, to feel deeply.

Our purpose is to immerse ourselves in each present moment, to meet it with an open heart, and to extend our hands to those in need. We are here to offer comfort to those in pain, to listen with compassion to their stories, and to understand their efforts to navigate a world that often seems to have lost its way. The willingness to care—doesn't need to be justified. It's a spark of our shared humanity.

Life will never be neat or complete. It's about embracing the unfinished edges, the mystery, and the imperfections. Our journey isn't about perfection but about presence—about carrying the light of our hearts into the world, just as the stars guide us through the night.

So let your heart be the light that never fades. Love, kindness, and understanding are sparks—like the stars—that light our paths and those we touch.

With Love and Hope

Lucy

1

Khalil's Desert Haven

From the stone house perched atop the hill, an unobstructed view of the mountain stretched out like a guardian of time. It was a warm summer evening in Zarifa, a rugged desert town where the battered earth found solace beside a majestic mountain, standing defiantly against the relentless ocean waves. The ceaseless surf mirrored decades of invasions, crashing as if to conquer the steadfast mountain, a metaphor for the quiet battles waged in the hearts of its inhabitants.

The desert embodied the energy that had worn away hope and tranquility, eroded by the sands of time. Yet hidden within its depths lay the most precious wealth: resilience. Similar to the hardy shrubs that dared to flourish in the harsh landscape, the people of Zarifa thrived against the odds. The land itself seemed a reflection of their existence, echoing both the threatening forces of nature and the inner struggles they faced. If one ever questioned the existence of such forces, the answer lay within.

Freedom, elusive and fervent, lay in the unrelenting struggle to break free from this place. Khalil often pondered this notion as he gazed at the mountains that embraced the horizon. His confines were often of his own making, shaped by love and responsibility. Without hope, life became a hollow vessel, and hope resided in the ability to envision happiness, while peace found its home in the chambers of the heart.

Amidst this backdrop, Khalil stood outside his home, known affectionately as Qasr Al Khalil—Khalil's Palace. The structure had been lovingly crafted from stone, its weathered walls adorned with family memories. A panama hat shielded him from the sun, while his bare feet sank into the warm earth, a comforting reminder of his roots. As he stirred the coals of his fire pit, he recalled his youth, filled with dreams of adventure and freedom, yet now anchored by a love that bloomed in the warmth of shared mornings and whispered secrets.

A bittersweet smile played upon his lips as he contemplated the whispers of an impending war. The distant murmur of discontent had reached his ears, carried on the wind like a specter. He cherished his life as it was—a life he was wary of altering. Saturdays were for lazy mornings, wrapped in each other's embrace until the sun was high. Sundays brought long baths shared with his beloved Rashida, followed by drifting into peaceful sleep beneath the soft warmth of a quilt.

Since his youth, he had been a guardian of all living things, his protective instinct extending to shield his wife from harm. Like all men, he appreciated life's pleasures—a fine glass of wine, the scent of smoked fish, the laughter shared over dinner. Why disrupt such harmony? In war, the victor is death, leaving everything else as mere casualties. Shaking off the somber thoughts, he gazed into the fire as if to banish them there.

On this tranquil night, stars emerged one by one, painting the desert sky with their brilliance. The scent of grilling meat wafted on the evening breeze, an enticing aroma that wrapped around everything. Khalil poured a dash of spice over the chicken skewers their colors bright against the golden flames. Did his desert home possess all modern-day comforts? Indeed, this neat dwelling boasted them all. Floor-to-ceiling shelves held a cherished collection of well-worn books, the titles whispering tales of distant lands and lost loves. The bar displayed an array of cognac, whiskey, and vodka, each bottle a reflection to celebratory moments shared with friends. The wine cellar was a treasure trove of French and Californian wines, aged to perfection, waiting for the right occasion.

Yet, amidst these modern comforts, the ancient tradition of a man cooking barefoot under the open sky persisted through the ages. This was the heartbeat of Zarifa—where the past and the present intertwined, creating a rich landscape of life.

"Dinner is served, my love," Khalil called, his voice warm and inviting. He arranged the chicken skewers on a plate, accompanied by a medley of fresh salad greens and flatbread, all prepared with love and care. As Rashida appeared, dressed in a pristine white linen dress that flowed like the gentle desert breeze, he planted a tender kiss upon her head. She was the light that brightened his darkest days, the anchor that steadied his restless heart.

Taking careful care, he pulled out her chair, and they sat down together. With a graceful gesture, he poured Merlot into two chilled glasses, the deep red liquid catching the light like liquid rubies. Soft melodies played in the background, blending harmoniously with the sounds of the desert night. Their happy conversation filled the air as they enjoyed their meal, laughter dancing between them like the stars above.

"What did you discover today, Khalil?" Rashida asked, her eyes sparkling with curiosity.

"Ah, I discovered that the stars seem closer when you're with someone you love," he replied, a playful grin spreading across his face.

"Perhaps they're jealous," she teased, nudging him playfully.

After dinner, they returned to the kitchen, a beautiful duet of two souls tidying up together. The clinking of dishes and the shared smiles echoed in the warm atmosphere. Khalil took pride in these small moments, where time slowed, and love filled the spaces in between.

Later, in his favorite rocking chair, Khalil puffed on his pipe, the fragrant smoke curling lazily into the air. Music filled the living area, soothing their souls as they relaxed in the comforting glow of the evening. Across the world, people shared common threads, holding the capacity to embrace life's richness and live it to the fullest. The thought brought him solace, reminding him of the shared human experience that transcended borders and conflicts.

As the night deepened, Khalil felt a flicker of unease tugging at his heart. The shadows of uncertainty loomed larger, and the whispers of war seemed to echo louder in the stillness. Yet, in this moment, surrounded by love and warmth, he chose to hold onto hope, believing in the power of resilience and the strength found within the human spirit.

"Tomorrow," he whispered, a tender smile gracing his lips, "let's walk down to the river. We can take a soft blanket, spread it out under the sun, and bask in its golden embrace, letting the world fade away around us."

Rashida smiled, her eyes twinkling. "I would love that."

And so, under the vast desert sky, they sat together, entwined in the knowledge that even in the face of adversity, love could be their sanctuary—a steadfast sanctuary against the storms that lay ahead.

2

A Love Wrapped in Twilight

The evening had transformed into a serene scene as the sun dipped below the horizon, casting a warm, orange glow across the sky. The fading daylight painted the world in dusky blues and oranges, with the first stars beginning to twinkle timidly. A gentle breeze rustled the leaves of nearby trees, carrying with it the sweet scent of blooming flowers. The air was cool and crisp, providing a refreshing contrast to the warmth of the day.

Nasser sat wrapped in the hush of twilight, the air alive with the gentle hum of crickets. The evening stretched around him, still and expectant, as he prepared to pour his heart onto the page. His love for Maya felt golden and fluid—warm, tender, and achingly fragile. He would have to guard it like the finest porcelain.

As the darkness deepened, it offered him solitude—a space where his emotions could unfurl freely. The soft glow of his table lamp turned the room into a sanctuary, cocooning him in warmth. His feelings stood like an ancient forest—deep-rooted, immense, unshakable. He saw nothing else, thought of nothing else.

The pen felt steady in his grip, and the blank page before him held a quiet promise—the chance to bridge the distance between his heart and Maya's. With a breath, he began to write.

My Love Maya,

As I sit here, the world outside cloaked in the soft embrace of twilight, my heart is filled with thoughts of you. I find myself wishing that I could sweep you away to Paris tonight. I imagine us at a charming café, where candlelight flickers and champagne sparkles with the promise of joy. With a bouquet of exquisite flowers before you, I'd share all those little moments and dreams that bring smiles to our hearts.

The thought of leaving weighs heavily on me, but I want you to keep the love I carry for you. It's a part of me, an unbreakable bond that runs through my veins. I believe that tonight could have been extraordinary if I were there to tell you this in person. You would have seen the tenderness in my eyes, and perhaps your tears would have softened my resolve to leave without you. How I yearn to explore the world by your side, yet the unpredictable nature of our lives calls for you to stay in Daryana, where it's safe.

Life has a way of surprising us, reshaping our paths without warning. What once felt certain can shift in an instant. We move through constant change, caught between its beauty and its weight. Some moments arrive like an unexpected breeze, while others cut through us with sharp and silent force.

It is hard to carry on as if nothing has changed when weapons line the streets of Zarifa and fear lingers in every shadow. Conflict does not just disrupt life—it alters the very shape of the road ahead. No signs warn of how far it has spread, no gentle turns soften its course. The path stretches forward, unyielding, shaped by forces beyond our control. Even the birds soar at a distance, untouched by the turmoil below.

And yet, even in the midst of such uncertainty, we keep moving. We search for light in darkness, for hope where it feels distant. Because change, even in its harshest form, cannot take away our will to keep going.

What kind of life is this, to exist under the constant shadow of uncertainty? How can we dream, plan, or look toward the future when fear lingers, pressing against us without cause? In a world where peace feels fragile, we long for the quiet assurance of safety—the freedom to live on our land without fear or hesitation.

Who knows when the troops will leave? Who knows when we will be free to truly live again? But we must find a way to go on. I don't know what the future holds, but I know this—I carry you with me. No distance can take away what we have. Though I must go, my heart remains with you. Hold on to hope, just as I do. This is not the end of our story, only a pause. And no matter what, we will find our way back to each other.

I do not know how to move forward, where to pause, or when to stop. Yet, somewhere deep inside, hope lingers—quiet, waiting. We need each other more than ever. No matter the path we take, I am forever by your side. But the weight of waiting for this war to end is unbearable. My deepest fear is for your safety, and that fear compels me to embark on this journey alone. We have no alternative, my love. The pull to explore—this quiet yet undeniable urge—is both a whisper and a force. It stirs a deep longing within, a gentle ache to uncover the extraordinary. And in time, I believe we find ourselves unfolding into a life that is richer, fuller, and more deeply attuned to the essence of who we are.

Understand, Maya, I am not choosing to leave you behind. My love for you remains unwavering. I will return for you, my beloved. No dream is complete without you in it.

We cannot retreat from life; instead, we must step into it fully, even in uncertainty. Trust that every step I take brings me closer to you, and every moment apart only deepens my devotion. Together, we will face the unknown with strong and unafraid hearts, knowing that love, in its purest form, always leads us back to where we belong. Until then, hold onto the belief that our story is far from over—it is just beginning.

Always yours,
Nasser

Nasser's Introspection

After finishing the note, Nasser found himself ensnared by an overpowering fear that seemed to constrict his very heart, its relentless pounding echoing in his chest. The notion of not having Maya by his side clawed at his soul, an unbearable thought that he had kept at bay, tucked away in the darkest recesses of his mind until now. At twenty-eight years old, he had never allowed himself to envision a life without her, their souls woven together for as long as he could remember.

The decision he was now contemplating weighed upon him like an immeasurable burden, casting a shadow of anguish across his entire being. It was a decision that would usher in a pain neither of them had ever known, a heartache so profound that it seemed to seep into his very bones. Nasser had always prided himself on being the protector, the one who shielded Maya from life's harsh realities. But now, he faced the harsh reality that, in some twisted way, he might be the source of her impending sorrow. Every moment spent pondering this decision felt like a relentless storm within him, thunderous doubts, and lightning flashes of uncertainty. He had always been their anchor, and yet, the anchor was adrift in a tempestuous sea of emotions. The weight of his choices bore down on him, and the turmoil within him threatened to consume him entirely.

Nasser couldn't help but replay the memories of their time together, like a film reel in his mind. The laughter, the shared dreams, the whispered promises, all entwined into the fabric of their love. Each cherished moment only intensified the crushing fear that he might be the one to unravel it all. The thought of a future without her felt like a gaping hole, an abyss of despair that threatened to swallow him whole. He knew that he was standing on a precipice, his choices leading him towards an unknown abyss. Yet, the pain of not having her by his side was matched only by the torment of causing her pain. His love for Maya was an unbreakable bond, but now, that very love had become the source of his greatest turmoil.

"Surely, we've faced challenges before," he thought, trying to convince himself. The sense of powerlessness lingered, but his resolve had solidified. "I am certain of this decision now."

Putting the note aside, he retrieved his guitar from its stand, his fingers tracing over the familiar strings. With a few deft adjustments, he began to strum, the harmonious notes filling the room. Each chord resonated within him, a soothing balm for his restless thoughts.

Lost in the melody, Nasser's mind drifted, the music allowing him to explore the depths of his emotions. The night outside was still a reflection of the calm before a storm. His contemplations looped back, replaying his internal struggle. "Perhaps some might call me foolish, but in truth, I am a dreamer," he acknowledged softly. "A dreamer who envisions a future with Maya."

He let his fingers dance across the strings, conjuring a soft, melancholic melody. It was the kind of tune that invited introspection, allowing thoughts to drift freely. And so, amidst the quiet chords, Nasser's mind wandered.

"A grand house with a sprawling garden and children, that is what I yearn for," he mused softly. "Maya and I have intertwined our lives together, anchored by this shared dream."

Memories of their journey together flickered in his mind's eye. The past was a compilation of shared experiences and whispered promises. "But now, uncertainty has cast its shadow," he acknowledged, his voice a mere whisper against the backdrop of his music. The world around them was shifting, transforming, and their once clear path had become shrouded in fog.

"I can't imagine my life without her," Nasser confessed, his fingers faltering briefly on the strings. The struggle within him was palpable—staying was heart-wrenching yet leaving seemed insurmountable. "I want to slip away quietly, without causing a stir," he sighed, his heart heavy with the weight of the decision.

He strummed a sequence of chords, the harmony echoing his turmoil. "Promises were made, vows to stay together forever," he murmured. "And I intend to keep mine."

The complexity of life's unanswered questions loomed, casting a shadow on his thoughts. "Life is intricate," Nasser concluded, his voice tinged with a mixture of resignation and wonder. "There are aspects we can't quite grasp, elements slipping through our fingers like sand."

He gazed at the guitar for a moment before continuing, "Something within us resists change, yearns for stability. Yet change is a constant companion, unpredictable as the wind." The notion of change unsettled him, for it often arrived without warning, upending even the firmest convictions.

As his fingers traced the strings once more, Nasser's voice turned reflective. "My loved ones are all here," he whispered, the vulnerability of his words hanging in the air. "The familiar is reassuring, yet change sneaks in, altering perceptions and beliefs."

His fingers danced on the strings; each note a fragment of his inner monologue. "Why this urge to leave the lakeside of my youth?" he wondered aloud, a rhetorical question laden with the weight of uncertainty. "Was the vast world created to lure us from our roots?"

"Distance and time conspire," he continued, his voice carrying a mix of sadness and resignation. "They subtly reshape and separate, quietly shifting like the changing seasons."

With a final chord, Nasser let the music fade into the silence of the room. He leaned back, his thoughts a tangle of emotions. "The world keeps turning, and so do we," he murmured. "But through it all, my bond with Maya remains unbroken. We are navigators of invisible paths, exploring the uncharted territories of our lives."

As Nasser set his guitar aside, the final notes still lingering in the air, he felt a profound sense of clarity wash over him. The twilight outside had deepened into night, stars now boldly adorning the sky, mirroring the flickers of hope and love within his heart. He knew the path ahead was fraught with uncertainty, yet in the quiet sanctuary of his room, illuminated by the soft glow of the table lamp, he found solace in his resolve.

His love for Maya was a compass, guiding him through the uncharted territories of life and war. It was a bond that neither time nor distance could sever, a promise embedded into the very fabric of his being. As he closed his eyes, Nasser envisioned a future where they would be reunited, their dreams once again intertwined.

In the stillness of the evening, with the world outside hushed in anticipation, Nasser made a silent vow. No matter the storms that lay ahead, he would return for Maya. For theirs was a love that transcended the boundaries of time and space, a love that would endure the darkest of nights and the brightest of days.

3

Love and Conflict

Nasser was merely seventeen when Maya first began attending his mother's studio for music lessons. Every Thursday, he waited with unwavering anticipation for her arrival. Her presence seemed to illuminate the studio, her laughter, a melody that lingered long after she left. During the subsequent spring festival, their connection deepened as they shared rides and experiences, eventually becoming inseparable. The mere touch of Maya's hand or a gaze into her eyes spoke volumes, expressing the profound love Nasser held for her.

Between spoken words and unspoken intentions lies a vast territory often unexplored, lost in translation. Love, much like art, embodies a gap between our aspirations and reality. Nasser felt a sense of unease as he considered the inevitable need to change his approach to maintaining their closeness. Any long-distance relationship poses challenges. Despite the apparent fulfillment of his life in Daryana—where he earned a comfortable livelihood and awaited the prospect of marrying the beautiful Maya—an incomprehensible desire to leave tugged at him. He wished with all his heart that he did not have to stand on the edge of this crossroad.

Zarifa's historical records were marred by numerous invasions, forcing its inhabitants to rebuild anew time and again. Nasser contemplated the years that might pass, marked by regretful pondering over his hesitations and the inexplicable choices he never pursued. He envisioned a life haunted by the question of why he didn't seize the opportunity, a thought he knew would be difficult to forgive himself for.

Frustration gripped Nasser as he reflected on how the war's stifling presence had impacted his decisions. Weighing his options, he confronted the dilemma. Departing might bar his return due to the conflict with the nearby Zarifa airport potentially closed off. The only alternative lay five hours away across the border, a risky journey for Maya. Amid sighs and contemplation, he clung to the hope that the war's turbulence would eventually subside. He planned to carve out a secure space and request Maya's hand in marriage from her father.

Although other girls at the hospital where he worked harbored feelings for him, none resonated with Nasser. Tearfully, he acknowledged that justification for his decision to leave held little weight. The war had come to dominate their lives, and he'd already resolved to depart.

Situated a considerable two hundred miles from the capital city's turmoil, Zarifa, Daryana retained its own unique allure. In Daryana, it had become customary for the youth to pursue higher education in Europe, cultivating a cultural blend as foreign partners returned. This infusion ushered in fresh ideas, fashion, cuisine, and narratives. However, the war disrupted ambitious plans, even affecting the development of a new shopping mall. Renowned for its olives, goats, and a variety of fruits—dates, peach, figs, and more—Daryana's Main Street was a combination of high-end boutiques, elegant eateries, charming cafés, a quintessential French bakery, a chocolate haven, and the traditional Shisha lounges. These lounges enticed people to relish the festive, laid-back ambiance while indulging in tobacco from ornate water pipes. The traditional essence of Daryana, embodied by centuries-old bread-makers and bustling souk markets, persisted alongside these modern additions. Situated at the crossroads of East and West, the region remained perplexed by a history of wars that left it in constant flux.

During the spring festival, the customary Shisha lounges, adorned with their traditional seating and vibrant melodies, once hosted patrons from distant lands. They reveled and mingled with locals until dawn. Yet, recent fear of the war's encroachment led to a decline in visitors. Nevertheless, the spring festival endured, defying the threatening backdrop. Daryana's inhabitants convened, reveling in laughter, music, dance, and shared joy.

Zarifa's skyline underwent metamorphosis in the early 1980s, with skyscrapers, a grand opera house crowned by a dome, a sprawling convention center, opulent hotels, and sprawling malls reshaping its identity. Beneath the night sky, people congregated around melodious fountains, and a towering Burj offered panoramic vistas until midnight. The architectural panorama mirrored Zarifa's rich heritage, where the Sultan's palace had evolved into a modern museum, celebrating the opulence of bygone eras. A modern airport facilitated global tourism, though the invasion had drastically altered this landscape. Nowadays, most shops bore a disheartening sign: "Closed Indefinitely."

In the heart of Zarifa, a profound change was happening, one that would alter its history forever. Foreign soldiers had arrived, their presence casting a shadow over the once lively city. The clank of their metal boots on the cobblestone streets announced their arrival, and their foreign banners waved ominously in the wind, starkly contrasting with the colorful tapestries that once decorated the city's buildings. These soldiers, faceless and clad in uniforms bearing unfamiliar military badges, carried with them an air of authority that chilled the hearts of Zarifa's inhabitants. Fear and uncertainty spread like wildfire through the city, as families huddled together behind locked doors and shuttered windows, their daily routines shattered by the intrusion.

As the foreign soldiers took over Zarifa, their orders were barked out in a harsh tongue, incomprehensible to the locals. They established checkpoints at key intersections, effectively paralyzing the flow of daily life. Marketplaces, once bustling with the vibrant exchange of goods and laughter, fell silent as merchants abandoned their stalls. The city's cafes, where stories and dreams were shared over cups of steaming tea, now stood empty.

Homes were raided, their occupants forced to submit to invasive searches, their possessions scrutinized by the intruders. Walls that had once heard the laughter of children and the melodies of music now echoed with the oppressive presence of foreign soldiers, their heavy boots trampling the sacred spaces of Zarifa's residents.

The foreign soldiers seemed to care little about the rich heritage of Zarifa's culture and history. Libraries and archives were ransacked, precious manuscripts torn and discarded. Works of art that had adorned the city's galleries for generations were seized and carted away, leaving empty spaces on the walls that once told stories of the city's past.

But amidst the darkness and despair, a glimmer of hope began to emerge. The people of Zarifa, resilient and united by a common purpose, found solace in one another. They whispered their defiance in hushed tones, vowing to protect their heritage and their way of life. Secret meetings were held in hidden corners of the city, where plans were hatched, and a spirit of resistance was born.

In Zarifa, a profound transformation had indeed occurred, but it was not solely one of domination and despair. It was also a transformation of resilience, unity, and determination. The foreign soldiers may have taken control of the city's streets, but they could not extinguish the flame of hope that burned in the hearts of its people. Zarifa would endure, and in time, it would rise once more, a tribute to the indomitable spirit of its inhabitants.

Centuries of feuds had compelled people to wander, carrying fragments of their homeland—soil and water—across vast expanses. Their journey's end culminated in a settlement, with Daryana enticing some with its familiarity. The Synagogue, Catholic Church, and Mosque that graced the landscape bore tribute to the coexistence of diverse faiths that thrived here. The town square of Daryana encapsulated the region's rich history in its symbolism. Here, religion didn't define people; instead, they gathered under the afternoon shade, sharing hookah pipes, sipping homemade lemonade, and engaging in conversations about the simple joys of life – books, tobacco, fishing, and the essence of harmony. Neighbors freely exchanged homemade bread, pickles, and fresh garden vegetables, nurturing a sense of unity that contrasted starkly with the turmoil plaguing the capital city. While the world assumed it was a religious conflict, unbeknownst to them, the true cause of the strife was the battle among capitalists from so-called "democratic" nations, vying for control over Zarifa's natural resources. The invasion came as a shock, as modern conflicts were expected to be limited to business deals where profits could be negotiated.

In the heart of Daryana, love and care flourished beyond imagination. Lifelong neighbors aged together, having attended the same schools, speaking languages that intertwined seamlessly – Arabic, Hebrew, and English. They shared recipes passed down through generations and carried names indigenous to the region. Even if not fully fluent in Arabic or Hebrew, they could effortlessly follow conversations. Life's milestones, whether weddings or births, were collective celebrations. Every blessing was appreciated, and gratitude filled the air for the abundance and kindness that enriched their lives. On Fridays, men often gathered at the Shisha lounge, a tradition that united them.

Daryana boasted its own distinct customs, highlighted during the area's spring festival. People from distant corners of the globe flocked to witness the festivities, admiring the local women, dancing, and reveling until dawn painted the sky. Along the lakeside, visitors strolled leisurely, basking in the sun's warmth, while cedarwood trees, planted years ago, formed a picturesque border. The desire to linger in this idyllic setting forever lingered in the hearts of these visitors.

Once upon a time, Zarifa, too, was a haven of tranquility. Its residents, irrespective of their religious affiliations, coexisted harmoniously. However, the tides turned with the onset of war. The turmoil in Zarifa cast a long shadow, influencing decisions even in Daryana. The war's widespread presence stifled the once carefree spirit, leaving many yearning for its end, hoping to reclaim the lost vibrancy of life. Traveling to Zarifa became a perilous endeavor, with the main airport's unpredictability shunned due to safety concerns.

Amid these shifts, Nasser found himself grappling with a growing sense of confinement. Bearing his grandfather's name, he was an only child, having spent much of his formative years traveling alongside his beloved parents. Their wisdom sculpted his worldview, and upon their return to Daryana, they deemed it best for Nasser to complete his higher education there. His heart resonated deeply with Daryana; he aspired to mirror his parents' life. Following in his father's footsteps, he pursued a medical degree at the university bordering Daryana.

Nasser's upbringing reflected the love shared by his parents, Samir and Nura. They had embraced a nomadic life, a journey that ultimately led them to settle permanently in Daryana. Samir, who had studied at a British university, met his Egyptian wife, Nura, during his academic pursuits. Their marriage was a powerful symbol of love transcending cultural boundaries. Nasser's connection to his parents was profound; he admired their bond and their unwavering way of life.

With Samir's establishment of a medical practice and Nura's music studio in Daryana, they rooted themselves firmly in the community. The lakeside home they built exuded elegance, featuring indoor and outdoor Jacuzzis for varying weather and an infinity pool for scorching summers. The lush back garden played host to countless celebrations.

Nasser's mother, with her artistic touch, had transformed their home into a haven of warmth and creativity. She adorned the walls with intricate tapestries and filled the rooms with the soothing melodies of traditional songs. Her love for teaching extended beyond the classroom, as she imparted stories and traditions that shaped their identity.

Their life was a harmonious blend of tradition and modernity. Evenings were spent gathered around the kitchen table, savoring dishes that blended flavors from Arabic cuisine and an array of international influences. Nasser's parents had built a life rooted in love, respect, and the values that had been passed down through generations.

Weekends were often spent by the lake, where Nasser strummed his guitar, indulged in canoeing, swam in the cool waters, and witnessed sunsets that painted the sky with delicate hues. The affection Samir and Nura shared was visible in their embraces and kisses, creating a warm cocoon that enveloped Nasser.

But as the war encroached on their idyllic existence, Nasser's heart grew heavy with uncertainty. The decision to leave, to protect the ones he loved, weighed heavily on his mind. He knew that the path ahead was fraught with challenges, yet he held onto the hope that they would one day return to the life they had cherished.

In the depths of his heart, Nasser carried the memories of his family's love, the laughter that had once filled their home, and the vibrant garden that had been their sanctuary. As he prepared to embark on a journey into the unknown, he vowed to preserve these precious memories and to carry the spirit of his family with him, no matter where the path led.

Reflecting on this cherished time, Nasser realized how fortunate he was to have experienced such a deep connection with his parents. In an age of busy schedules and absentee parenthood, he recognized the rarity of his upbringing. Life often unfolds in monotonous cycles of obligations, leaving little room for genuine enjoyment. Nasser resolved to prioritize family, longing to nurture a close bond with his own children.

4

Beyond Borders: Hope, love, Dreams

Standing up, Nasser gently placed his guitar in its designated spot, contemplating the decisions ahead. He considered what to pack, discarding medical journals—echoes of practices that were evolving too quickly. His gaze landed on a bookshelf brimming with memories. "The Adventures of Blackbird" stood out, a relic from his London days, reminding him of the chapters that had shaped him. Though worn with age, its story still resonated, unlike the other books he cleared from his shelves.

As he reorganized his room, a narrative from his childhood replayed in his mind: "A blackbird soared above the hills. This world knows no bounds," the blackbird thought, gliding effortlessly. "How did this all begin, and where shall it end? I am but a speck on creation's canvas." From its lofty perch, the bird observed the myriad paths crisscrossing the gentle slopes. Did all these routes converge upon a singular destination?

It felt liberated as it chased its heart's yearnings. Over eastern and western hills, the bird journeyed, realizing it was merely a guest on Earth. Leaving each day behind, it understood the futility of looking back. Embracing new paths daily, it learned to relish the scenery without assumptions or expectations. Wisdom blossomed from past errors. In tranquil silence, understanding deepened, and through steadfast perseverance, it unearthed its inner strength. Its self-assurance flourished. Though the unknown loomed mysteriously, the dread of it proved unfounded. One certainty prevailed: sweetness infused every berry, wherever it grew.

The blackbird's senses sharpened in new surroundings; danger's scent was discernible. Omens lingered in the air, serving as warnings. Yet, some perils remained unavoidable despite caution. Hardships concealed themselves in inexplicability. Brutal storms and fierce winds defied reason, much like the origin of suffering remained a mystery untouched by logic. They astonished, thrusting one unexpectedly into their midst, but they nurtured growth in ways beyond understanding. Embracing the unknown required courage, while enduring it demanded perseverance. In strange lands, the bird encountered unfamiliar creatures—some hostile, others fierce. It faced challenges head-on, discovering its own strength, endurance, and limits.

Over time, it learned to communicate through humor and song, easing tensions and forging friendships. Its purpose became clear: to spread joy through storytelling. Each tale concluded with a reminder to embrace life's richness and seek genuine connections. Here, shared desires for love, laughter, and companionship united them all. "Embrace the journey, for it whispers of unexpected connections and untapped possibilities waiting to unfold."

Out of nowhere, a wise old bird remarked, "Did you think you were just picking berries? As we focus on one thing, something unexpected happens. That's how the Wise Ones work. We start one thing, and another unfolds. That's our destiny, the mysterious force guiding us."

Nasser found himself annoyed by the ongoing mental chatter. Thoughts of Paris' allure and charm drifted through his mind, stirring conflicting emotions. He knew his mother, Nura, would express both concern and joy upon hearing his news. "I'll arrange for Mama to visit Maya soon after I leave. Her support will help Maya understand." With that decision made, he packed essentials, took a quick shower, and rested. Under the gentle gaze of a new moon, sleep finally found him, perhaps symbolizing new beginnings.

The next day dawned early, and Nasser found himself at his father's clinic, the air thick with anticipation. He intended to share his plans, but the weight of his decision felt almost crushing. As he began to speak, his voice wavered, haunted by the thought of leaving without a final glimpse of Maya. The mere idea of it was unbearable. After a brief silence, he turned to Samir, his heart heavy. "The situation in Zarifa has taken a toll on me. I want to build a life in Paris that will make Maya eager to join me when the time comes. We can return to Daryana when the moment is right. The experience at the international hospital will be invaluable. I trust I can count on your support."

Samir understood his son well; Nasser's decisions were always careful and deliberate. The turmoil of war had obscured the essence of life. Samir's worry about his son's safety seemed unnecessary; he shouldn't let his concerns stand in the way of Nasser's determination. Nasser looked tired, reflecting on the difficulty of his decision. The day surged forth, a whirlwind of preparations—packing, flights, even a police escort for safety to Zarifa. A Paris hotel reservation confirmed his sense of fleeing. Soon, he would call Maya upon his arrival. A feeling of being a fugitive nestled within him.

That night, Papa Samir took pen to paper, his heart heavy with emotions that only a father's love could conjure. His words flowed onto the page with a tenderness that only time and experience could impart.

"My Dearest Son," he began, the ink tracing the curves of each letter as if they were a map to his feelings. "I write to you about the remarkable journey of life and to convey the depth of my love for you. Youth is a season filled with countless moments, both day and night, waiting to unravel the mysteries that life holds. Within you lie seeds of potential, eager for the moment they can blossom into something extraordinary."

"Life's treasures are vast, but they demand the courage to break the limits that hold us back and allow life's greatness to reveal itself. I've come to realize that our true potential emerges from the trials and challenges life presents." Amidst the quiet of the night, Samir's thoughts shifted to a distant memory—a warm summer morning in Daryana, when he had embarked on a journey to London. The full moon still clung to the sky, its radiant beauty offering no solace to the ache in his heart. Leaving a piece of himself behind, he journeyed onward.

"Time is a fleeting companion," he reflected, allowing his pen to dance across the page. "Each day slips away like grains of sand—grasp them tightly, savoring their warmth. Find joy in the beauty of every petal, every crashing wave, every storm, every creature, and the soft caress of sunlight. The answers to life's great mysteries are nestled within its sacred beauty. I came to understand this truth while listening to the whisper of a delicate leaf—one that, much like us, endures storms and hardships, only to revel in the vibrant warmth of summer after winter's chill. Embrace the myriad facets of life, for together they compose the intricate melody of our existence."

Samir's words echoed with urgent clarity as he shared his philosophy on embracing life's unpredictable nature. "Life doesn't pause for the perfect moment. Nature moves to its own rhythm, undeterred by the circumstances surrounding it. Even in the stillness, storms can arise without warning. The unknown stretches beyond our understanding.

Faith, then, is about acknowledging that there are dimensions we simply can't grasp."

He shifted to the essence of the matter, speaking to the relentless pull of personal desires and dreams. "Our hearts are like cosmic magnets, drawing us toward the next chapter of our journey. True courage lies in our willingness to take risks and navigate uncharted territory, guided by our inner compass. The world will always present its challenges, but dreams are borne from the strength of our determination. Amid life's ebbs and flows, cling to your dreams—they are the architects of your future."

With fatherly wisdom, he tackled the complexities of love and relationships. "Love flourishes not through sacrifice or compromise alone. Growth, evolution, and changing desires are inherent to our nature. Love should never strangle personal growth. Instead, let it breathe, allowing it to adapt and thrive amidst change. Maya, a remarkable presence in our lives, deserves every bit of our affection, even if circumstances prevent her from accompanying you. As Rumi aptly put it, 'Lovers don't finally meet somewhere. They're in each other all along.'"

Samir's thoughts drifted back to the tranquility of their hometown, Daryana, where time flowed gently, and simple joys held great significance. "In Daryana, life's pace is gentle, allowing room for what truly matters—be it canoeing, fishing, or simply basking in the symphony of nature. Such moments paint life's canvas with serenity."

But the tone shifted as he confronted the harsher realities of the world, a world embroiled in the conflict of men over resources in Zarifa. "War has cast a shadow, upending the world as we knew it. This war is a harsh interruption, reshaping our existence and constraining our liberties. Within limitations, we catch a glimpse of the impending need for change before it materializes."

Samir's letter transformed into a narrative about navigating foreign lands and cultures, an exploration of how to hold onto one's identity amid external pressures. "A foreign land can change you in profound ways. Work becomes a delicate balancing act, requiring you to juggle responsibilities, seize opportunities, and push beyond your comfort zones. Your unique heritage sets you apart, inviting curious questions about your background, your cuisine, and even the way you prepare scrambled eggs. Yet, the weight of expectation can feel heavy, urging you to conform."

As he delved deeper into his journey, Samir addressed the challenge of maintaining individuality in a world that often values conformity. "People will impose their ideals upon you, questioning your choices. But there is no need to live in fear of losing yourself to their perspectives. Yes, the world may reject you for your uniqueness but meet each challenge with an open heart. Your heart knows when to forge ahead and when to pause. The cost of freedom is worthwhile, for true freedom lies in overcoming those barriers."

The tone of the letter shifted to reflect perseverance and the pursuit of personal goals. "The true test lies in enduring and realizing one's ambitions. Some of my contemporaries faltered, unable to withstand the weight of change. They left feeling defeated, only to eventually reconnect, their reunion forged from the wise threads of time and the evolution of understanding."

Samir's reflections then turned to the interplay between work, happiness, and success. "Society often equates success and happiness with wealth and ambition. But fulfillment is far more intricate than mere material gain. I envision a world where parents speak of their children's happiness in pursuing their passions and creative endeavors. May those journeys lead to both prosperity and contentment."

In the quiet shadows of the night, Samir's thoughts drifted to the enduring strength of love. "I envision a world where love remains as steady as the rhythm of day and night," he mused. Maya's presence enriches our lives, and though distance may separate you, our affection remains unwavering. I long for the day when your paths will unite again."

The letter drew to a close with an embrace of life's mysteries and a father's steadfast love. "Go forth, my son, and uncover your purpose. Life's depths are unfathomable. Always keep the lovely Maya close to your heart. Our dreams wrap around your return and future family. Take all the time you need to find your way; my pride in you is boundless."

The signature, "Love you always, Dad," symbolized a father's unwavering support through life's mysterious journey.

The morning sun unfurled its golden arms, painting the world in colors of promise and warmth, yet all Nasser could feel was a shadow deep within, a storm cloud that dulled the day's brilliance. Doubt clawed at his heart, unraveling the threads of determination he had spun so carefully. "Maybe I should just leave now, while my courage still flickers," he thought, the weight of fatigue draping over him like an unwelcome blanket, a restless night having siphoned away his strength.

To his surprise, the police escort arrived early, whisking him away before he could indulge in a leisurely breakfast or savor a lingering goodbye. Nura stood before him, her eyes shimmering with unshed tears, enveloping him in a farewell hug that spoke volumes—love, longing, and the heartache of separation.

Samir, his father, mustered a brave smile, a facade that did little to mask his concern as he handed Nasser a letter, the paper imbued with unspoken words of wisdom and care. A gentle kiss brushed against Nasser's cheeks, a tender promise lingering in the air. "We'll find our way back to each other soon, my son," Samir whispered, the words both a comfort and a reminder of the journey ahead.

Settling into the back seat of the police car, Nasser watched as his parents faded into the distance, the vehicle carrying him away from everything familiar. Yet, as the scenery blurred by, his mind shifted to thoughts of Maya, punctuated by vivid memories of his childhood. He could almost feel the cool breeze from the lakeshore, hear the laughter that echoed through those sun-drenched afternoons. His mother, a gifted musician, had a gift for discerning the songs of birds, her voice a soothing balm. "Some sounds endure, unchanged," she would muse, her eyes bright with reverence. "These melodies were sung long before we were here, just as God's voice whispers to us when we are ready to listen. They resonate through eternity."

Her words hung in the air, wrapping around Nasser like a warm embrace, infused with nostalgia. But then his thoughts shifted back to Maya, and the ache of her absence settled in his chest, an ever-present reminder of love and longing intertwined.

He glanced around the car with a mix of hope and anxiety, as if silently pleading for a reason to turn back, to return to Maya. The journey to the airport felt charged, each moment thick with unspoken fears. Armed guards stood sentinel along the way, their expressions fierce, a constant reminder of the peril surrounding them.

Inside the police vehicle, an unsettling quietness enveloped them, draining the world of its vibrancy. The streets lay desolate; not even a stray dog dared to wander. The wind, once a playful companion, now carried a sorrowful melody, deepening the tension that made Nasser's skin prickle with unease. Each mile stretched into uncertainty, amplifying his longing for the familiar, a comfort that felt impossibly out of reach.

As they approached the final checkpoint before the airport terminal, the atmosphere thickened with suspense. Security was at its most vigilant, every movement scrutinized with a hawk-like intensity. It was as if the air itself held its breath, ready to snap at the slightest hint of trouble.

But then, as Nasser stepped onto the aircraft, a wave of relief swept over him like a cool breeze on a sweltering day. The plane, though only sparsely populated, offered a sanctuary, a brief reprieve from the looming shadows outside. As the engines roared to life, he felt the weight of his worries begin to lift, each sound a promise of escape.

Settling into his seat, he embraced the mix of excitement and lingering anxiety. The gentle hum of the aircraft's engines vibrated through him, a comforting signal of the journey ahead. His thoughts spiraled back to the essence of Daryana, the enduring legacy of his parents, filled with love and wisdom, accompanying him on this voyage. The warmth of the seat pressed against his back felt reassuring, a tangible reminder that he was on a path infused with purpose, destined for new experiences and profound connections waiting just beyond the horizon.

5

In The Shadow of Uncertainty

As the morning sun filtered softly through the curtains, Nura gently lifted a ruby and diamond ring from her ornate trinket box. This ring was her most cherished possession, a gift from her husband, Samir—a symbol of love bought during their early days in London, long before they were married. In those moments, she felt like the center of his universe. Samir wasn't just a spouse; he was her confidant, her best friend. Her father, Nasser, a renowned Egyptian archaeologist, had once told her, "A wedding ceremony does not make a marriage." Yet, he saw in Samir the same qualities she valued—a source of comfort.

As Nura polished the ring, a tender reminder of Samir's enduring love, she felt a wave of nostalgia wash over her. Memories of shared laughter and whispered secrets filled her mind, warming her heart against the cool touch of the present.

Later that morning, Nura walked to Maya's house, crossing a bridge over a serene lake. Despite the sun's warmth, a slight chill hinted at the changing season. Overhead, ospreys circled gracefully, their unwavering focus captivating Nura's attention as she pondered her own resolve. The birds' determination mirrored her inner thoughts, each flap of their wings echoing a silent promise to stay strong.

At the threshold of Maya's home, Zataar, their loyal adopted dog, bounded forward with unrestrained joy, his tail wagging in a rhythm of pure happiness. His eyes sparkled with a warmth that spoke volumes, reflecting the unconditional love he had found here. Nura, witnessing this touching scene, felt a pang of empathy for the countless animals left to fend for themselves amid the chaos of war. She knelt down, wrapping her arms around Zataar, feeling his sturdy frame lean into her, seeking the solace that only a loving touch can provide. In that moment, she marveled at the dog's profound ability to sense and respond to the essence of human goodness.

Stepping into the cozy embrace of Maya's home, Nura couldn't help but feel a wave of comfort wash over her. "Maya," she began, her voice filled with genuine warmth, "it's always so wonderful to see you."

"And you, my dear Nura. Come, let's have some coffee," Maya replied, leading her to the cozy glass porch. The aroma of freshly brewed Arabic coffee filled the air, offering warmth and solace as emotions simmered just below the surface, hinting at the storm that was yet to come.

"Nadia should be back from the gym soon," Maya mentioned, pouring the coffee.

Nura took a deep breath, her heart heavy with the weight of what she was about to reveal. She gently unveiled a small box from her purse, feeling the moment's gravity. "Maya, what I'm about to share might catch you off guard," she began, opening the box to reveal an exquisite ring. "This ring is for you."

Maya's eyes widened, reflecting surprise and confusion. "For me? Nura, it's beautiful! But why...?"

Nura smiled gently, her heart aching for Maya. "It's a symbol of love. Samir gave it as a promise of his love. Nasser's sudden departure for Paris may be hard to understand, but it's out of concern for your safety.

He felt compelled to leave, even though it meant leaving without you. Please understand, dear Maya, that you are not abandoned. Nasser intends to reunite with you in Paris."

Maya's voice trembled, the weight of Nura's words settling heavily in the air. "He left because of me?"

"No, not because of you," Nura reassured, placing a comforting hand on Maya's. "Because he loves you and wants to protect you. You mean the world to him."

Nura's words struck Maya like a lightning bolt, stirring intense emotions she couldn't quite contain. Normally, Maya found comfort in Nasser's love, but now it felt suffocating, trapping her in a whirlwind of doubt. Tears flowed silently down her cheeks, a silent reflection to the turmoil within her.

Nura hugged Maya tightly, their bond evident in the embrace. "We'll get through this together," she whispered. "You're not alone."

As Nura's arm draped over Maya's shoulder, radiating solidarity, a steadfast certainty emerged amidst the tears—an unbreakable bond forged through shared experiences that transcended time and adversity. Amid challenges, a whispered promise lingered—love, in all its forms, would guide them.

Nura hoped this initial reaction was transient. She understood the grip of trauma and how it could stifle one's spirit. The devastating loss of Maya's mother had left a profound wound, and Nura knew these inner barriers required Maya's strength to overcome. Even with love surrounding her, the journey to heal was one Maya had to navigate alone. Seeing a loved one struggle was deeply touching, making Nura wish for Maya to see the flicker of hope in the darkness.

"Maya, remember when you used to dream about your future over coffee just like this?" Nura said softly, her voice filled with warmth. "Those dreams haven't vanished. They're still within reach."

Maya nodded, wiping her tears. "I just feel so lost sometimes."

Nura understood how unhappiness could gradually dim life's brilliance. Doubt created barriers that suffocated trust and drained life of vitality. Yet, she believed in the resilience of the human spirit. She hoped Maya would find the strength to step beyond uncertainty and mend her wounded heart. Nura stood as a guardian, wishing for Maya to understand that even in the darkest times, there is potential for renewal and healing.

With a gentle exhalation, Nura acknowledged the road ahead might be strewn with obstacles. "Love can brighten even the darkest corners of the heart," she said softly. "You have to believe that."

Maya looked up, her eyes searching Nura's. "Thank you for being here."

"Always," Nura replied with a reassuring smile.

Just then, the sound of a car engine broke the silence. Nadia had arrived. Nura gave Maya reassuring kisses on her cheeks, her heart racing with the need to comfort Maya, before promising her return.

September brought a change in seasons, with a brisk autumn breeze stirring the leaves, whispering secrets of transformation. As Nura approached, Nadia noticed the urgency in her steps. In their quiet conversation, Nura shared the surprising news of Nasser's journey to Paris.

Concern etched itself on Nadia's face, her brow furrowing in reflection as she listened to Nura's worries.

"I'm really worried about Maya," Nura confided, the weight of her concern evident in her voice. "I just want to lift her spirits and be there for her through all this. Keep me posted on how she's doing, okay? If Maya is up to it, maybe tomorrow during lunch we can raise our glasses in a toast to celebrate Nasser's safe arrival in Paris."

Nadia nodded, her eyes filled with empathy. "Of course, Nura. I'll keep a close eye on her. She needs all the love and support we can give right now."

With a final hug for Zataar, Nadia's faithful dog, Nura said her goodbye. She left soft kisses on Nadia's cheeks, but as she turned to leave, a sense of foreboding settled over her like a heavy fog. "I hope Maya can hold on," she thought, her heart tightening at the uncertainty that lay ahead.

Nadia stood there, her whispering "Wow" caught in the wind's embrace. Leaves danced and twirled in the breeze, mirroring the whirlwind of emotions within her heart. Crossing the threshold into the house, her pulse quickened, the weight of uncertainty settling heavily upon her shoulders.

In the glass-enclosed porch, Maya sat, clutching the letter, tears tracing delicate trails down her cheeks. Nadia's heart swelled with empathy as she reached out, her touch bridging the gap between words and emotions.

"Maya, it's going to be alright," Nadia whispered gently. "Nasser hasn't abandoned you—he's just taking a step forward. True love is about nurturing and supporting each other. Trust in Nasser and allow him the space he needs. It's in that space where love can truly blossom and become even more beautiful."

Maya looked up, her eyes filled with sorrow. "But why now? Why leave when everything feels so uncertain?"

Nadia held Maya's hand, a silent pact of solidarity. "Sometimes, the hardest decisions are made out of love. Nasser is doing this for you, for your safety. And we'll get through this together."

Maya nodded, though doubt still lingered in the air like a heavy mist. "I know. It's just... I've seen people leave and never come back."

"The past haunts us, but Nasser is different," Nadia reassured her. "He loves you deeply, and that love will bring him back to you."

The words Nasser had penned in his letter were meant to convey his love and provide reassurance to Maya. Yet, instead of finding comfort in his words, they took root in her anxious mind, triggering fears that had been dormant since her childhood. Memories of her mother's death rose like a tide, igniting a wave of doubt that crashed against her heart. It was this doubt that held her captive, leaving her feeling paralyzed and lost. She closed her eyes, feeling it creep through her veins like a chilling poison, sapping her strength and casting shadows over her hope.

"What could be more unsafe than war?" she wondered aloud, her voice barely above a whisper. "War changes people."

Nadia squeezed her hand. "I know it does, but love has its own power. It can change us too; in ways we can't always see. Nasser's love for you is strong, and that will help him come back."

Seated together on the enclosed front porch, the two sisters shared a wordless companionship. While Maya was lost in her own contemplation, Nadia's mind wandered, a habit she had cultivated over the years. The tangible sounds of the wind rustling through the nearly bare trees, the sun descending in the west to cast its golden glow over the pale green hills, and the twilight hues painting the world with a soft brush—all of these went unnoticed as Maya's heart pulsed with unspoken fears.

"It's easy to become angry when faced with change," Maya mused, her sorrow over her mother's death finding an outlet in her sombre mood.

Nadia nodded, her eyes fixed on the ring adorning Maya's finger, a symbol of the love between her sister and Nasser. "Change is hard, but it's also a chance for transformation. Nasser's absence might feel like an eternity, but it's just a moment in the grand scheme of things."

Beyond the confines of the porch, the moon cast a gentle glow in the lonely expanse of the sky, followed by the hesitant appearance of stars. Nature, an exquisite artist, captured the moment in all its intricate details—the stars finally emerging to glisten in the melancholic night sky, a reminder of the beauty that still existed amidst despair.

"We'll look back on this time and see how strong we've become," Nadia said softly, her voice a balm against Maya's uncertainty. "And when Nasser returns, we'll be even stronger."

Maya sighed, a flicker of hope igniting within her as a small smile formed on her lips. "Thank you, Nadia. Your words mean a lot to me."

Nadia smiled back, the bond between them growing stronger with each passing moment. "Always, sister. Always."

But just as they settled into the comfort of their shared space, the distant sound of sirens echoed through the night, slicing through the calm. The sisters exchanged a look, their hearts racing, the unspoken question hanging heavily in the air: What now?

6

The Sisters Sanctuary

Sirens wailed through the streets, a haunting soundtrack piercing the stillness of dusk, echoing through the alleys like a distant lament. Each cry sent a shiver of dread through Nadia and Maya as they stood at the precipice of uncertainty, acutely aware of the fragile safety they clung to like a threadbare blanket against the chill of night.

"Do you think it's an ambulance?" Maya's voice trembled, betraying the fear bubbling beneath the surface, her eyes wide as saucers.

"Maybe. Or the police. It's hard to tell," Nadia replied, her heart heavy with longing for her father. "I wish Papa were here. He would know what to say."

The wail transformed the air around them, wrapping their hearts in a chilling embrace of urgency. It served as a stark reminder of the dangers lurking just beyond their doorstep, waiting patiently like shadows in the night.

Unlike her sister Maya, Nadia, who had just turned twenty-four, carried a quiet wisdom, the kind that comes from witnessing too much, too soon. Their father, with his soothing voice, would read poetry to them each night as they lay in bed. His words were like a warm blanket, a gentle enchantment warding off the encroaching darkness.

"Papa's presence feels like a magic spell," Maya whispered, her voice a fragile thread in the night. "I feel much safer when he's here."

Nadia chuckled softly, the sound a gentle balm amid the chaos. "His words still feel like magic. They make everything seem safe, even when it isn't."

The memory of their mother loomed large—a tragedy that left indelible marks on their souls. Nadia remembered the nights their father's voice faltered as he read, the words blurring through tears. It was those very words that inspired her to pursue creative writing, a light of hope in a world overshadowed by sorrow.

As she cradled her favorite cup filled with fragrant mint tea, Nadia's thoughts drifted to Nasser, the man who had captured Maya's heart. She whispered silent prayers for him, hoping for his safety and freedom. "I know Nasser wouldn't willingly cause harm," she murmured, her heart aching with empathy. "He must have left with a heavy heart."

"What if he never comes back?" Maya's voice was barely above a whisper, a tremor in her tone that mirrored her fear.

Nadia reached out, placing a reassuring hand on her sister's shoulder. "He will, Maya. He loves you. But we both know there's so much cruelty in the world. It's the uncertainty that gnaws at you, isn't it?"

Maya nodded, her emerald-green eyes glistening with unshed tears. "Sometimes I feel like I'm just waiting for the next bad thing to happen."

Nadia sighed, the weight of her sister's pain settling heavily on her heart. "It's a natural response to loss, but we can't let it consume us. You have to trust that there is beauty still left in the world."

"Beauty?" Maya echoed, skepticism threading through her words. "With war raging around us? It feels like beauty is a distant memory."

Nadia took a deep breath, seeking the right words. "Think of the children in Zarifa. A generation growing up in a culture that extinguishes anything perceived as a threat. My heart aches at the thought of these children never experiencing the simple joys of play, the enchantment of poetry, the thrill of singing, the warmth of gingerbread men, the excitement of a carnival, or even the innocence of collecting wildflowers. The stark reality of children dancing to the rhythm of bullets, using books as kindling for fires—no one seems to contemplate the cruelty of war and the extent of human suffering it inflicts. I can't help but wonder how these children will ever come to know the beauty that exists in the world. I shudder at the image of young ones evading soldiers, witnessing their friends being shot, and mothers wailing.

"They're growing up in a culture that sees life as disposable. They deserve joy—play, poetry, laughter. But war strips away their innocence. It's heartbreaking."

Maya's gaze softened, her vulnerability drawing Nadia in closer. "What if they grow up to only know pain?"

Nadia's heart ached at the thought. "Then we must show them that love can exist even in darkness. We need to believe that humanity can rise above this."

A memory of their father's wisdom floated through Nadia's mind: "Every event in your life serves a purpose. Trust it. Value your self-worth and treat yourself with tenderness."

"Do you think Nasser left because he didn't care?" Maya's voice quivered, a fragile thread of doubt.

"No, it's more complicated than that. If you're feeling abandoned, remember it's about you. It's your struggle." Nadia paused, contemplating her sister's inner turmoil. "You've both been through so much. It's okay to feel lost. But don't let it harden your heart."

"What if he finds someone else?" Maya's tone brimmed with desperation, the fear consuming her.

Nadia shook her head firmly, her voice steady like the beat of a drum. "Maya, you are beautiful, both inside and out. If he wanted someone else, he would have sought her out here. You are his home."

Maya's posture softened slightly, the tension easing as Nadia's words took root in her heart. "But what if he changes? What if he doesn't come back the same?"

"Then we adapt," Nadia replied, a steady calm infusing her words. "We hold onto hope and faith. Change doesn't have to mean loss. It can mean growth."

"Sometimes I feel like I'm fighting a battle with my own heart," Maya confessed, the weight of her struggle laid bare.

"Every challenge teaches us something," Nadia said, recalling her father's teachings. "It's about finding the strength to face life's uncertainties. And it's okay to lean on each other during these times."

Maya managed a small smile, a flicker of light in the shadows. "You're right. I just need to breathe and trust that he'll return."

"Exactly! Let's not dwell on fear. Instead, let's cook something together. It'll take our minds off everything," Nadia suggested, her eyes sparkling with enthusiasm, a reminder that even in the darkest moments, joy could still flicker to life.

"Dinner sounds good," Maya agreed, her spirit lifting, if only for a moment. Together, they would navigate the chaos, holding onto each other and the fragile hope that still blossomed in their hearts.

The pizza dough was prepared, its warm, yeasty aroma a comforting presence in the kitchen. Nadia expertly rolled it out, her hands steady and practiced, adding toppings with the care of an artist painting a canvas. The vibrant colors of fresh vegetables and fragrant herbs created a visual feast that promised solace amid uncertainty. Maya, however, remained distant, her mind adrift as she mechanically sliced a tomato for the salad. Each cut echoed the turmoil swirling within her, a rhythm that mirrored her racing thoughts.

As Nadia placed the finished pizza in the oven, the tantalizing aroma began to fill the air, mingling with the soft scent of herbs and the warmth of freshly baked bread. It was a comforting connection to home, a brief relief from the heaviness of their worries. Nadia poured two glasses of Merlot, the deep red liquid glinting in the soft light. With a sense of purpose, she redirected the conversation toward a more hopeful perspective.

"Nasser's time in Paris offers you a wonderful opportunity to audition for an orchestra there," she suggested gently, her tone encouraging. Nadia envisioned Maya pursuing her passion for music in a vibrant new environment. "Imagine playing in such a lively city! The possibilities are endless." Amidst the challenges, Nadia believed there could be silver linings, and by focusing on the bright horizon ahead, she hoped to uplift Maya's spirits and inspire her to embrace the journey with optimism.

As Nadia switched on their favorite playlist, familiar melodies drifted through the glass porch, wrapping around them like a warm embrace. The stars twinkled overhead, creating a stunning backdrop that was both beautiful and comforting. Despite the exhaustion from the emotional ups and downs of the day, the music infused the atmosphere with a sense of calm, as if the universe conspired to create a moment of respite from their tumultuous lives.

Yet, as they sat down at dinner, Maya struggled to contain her emotions. The weight of the day pressed heavily on her, and the urge to cry bubbled just beneath the surface, threatening to spill over. She forced a smile, trying to mask her inner turmoil, but Nadia could see the cracks in her facade. Throughout the day, Maya had hardly eaten; her appetite had been dampened by distress, each bite seeming to catch in her throat as she wrestled with her feelings.

"Maya, it's okay to feel overwhelmed," Nadia said softly, her eyes filled with concern. "You don't have to pretend to be strong all the time." She reached out, placing a comforting hand over Maya's, the warmth of her touch grounding them both.

Maya took a shaky breath, the weight of her emotions pressing against her chest like a physical force. "I just don't know what to do," she confessed, her voice barely above a whisper. "Everything feels so uncertain. What if Nasser doesn't come back? What if he forgets me?"

Nadia squeezed her hand gently. "He won't forget you. You have a bond that goes beyond distance. But it's okay to miss him. It's okay to grieve what you've lost." She paused, allowing her sister to absorb her words. "Remember, even in darkness, there's light to be found. We just have to look for it."

Maya's eyes glistened with unshed tears as she nodded, grateful for her sister's unwavering support. They shared a moment of silence, the music flowing around them, a gentle whisper of the wonder that still existed in the world.

As they finally began to eat, Nadia watched Maya closely, keenly aware of each bite she took. Though Maya's fork moved mechanically, there was a flicker of determination in her eyes. With every slice of tomato and every sip of wine, Nadia hoped that her sister would reclaim a piece of herself, one meal at a time.

After dinner, they cleared the table together, the simple act of washing dishes grounding them in the present moment. The aroma of pizza lingered in the air, a fragrant trace that life could still offer small pleasures.

"Would you like to shower first?" Nadia asked, her voice gentle and understanding, already anticipating the need to provide support to her sister.

"Thank you," Maya replied quietly, her voice barely above a whisper. As she climbed the stairs, tears began to stream down her face, the weight of her emotions becoming too heavy to bear.

In the privacy of the shower, Maya found solace, the sound of her sobs echoing in the bathroom as she allowed herself to release the pent-up emotions that had been building inside her. Despite the pain she felt, there was a sense of relief in letting go, even if just for a moment, knowing that she wasn't alone and that her sister was there.

Downstairs, Nadia remained in the kitchen, her heart aching for her sister. She busied herself with tidying up, the familiar tasks providing a semblance of normalcy. The bond of sisterhood and the enduring power of love would guide them through these dark times

As Nadia finished cleaning, she poured herself a cup of tea and sat at the kitchen table, allowing the warmth to seep into her hands. She knew that the journey ahead would be challenging, but she also knew that together, they could face anything. The love and resilience they shared would be their strength, their anchor in the storm.

When Maya finally emerged from the shower, her eyes red and puffy, Nadia greeted her with a tender smile and a warm embrace. No words were needed; the silence between them spoke volumes. In that quiet moment, they found solace in each other's presence, their hearts intertwined in a shared journey of resilience and love.

"Let's take it one day at a time," Nadia whispered, her voice filled with determination and hope.

Maya nodded, drawing strength from her sister's unwavering support. "Together," she replied, her voice steady despite the tears that still lingered.

Together, they would navigate the challenges ahead, holding onto the hope and love that had always guided them. Within the walls of their home, they had created a sanctuary of resilience, a reflection of the enduring power of sisterhood. And no matter what the future held, they knew that they would face it side by side.

7

The Hearts Compass

As Nadia wandered to another part of the house, she began to draw a bath, her mind adrift with reflections. Bath time always held a particular solace for her, and today was no exception. As the tub filled, she found herself thinking about Maya. In a quiet murmur, as if to herself, Nadia pondered aloud, "Yes, life is unpredictable; that's the essence of the human journey. We don't get a map or a guarantee, just the exhilarating adventure of not knowing what's coming next. When we pause to look inward and explore our emotions, we realize that our experiences, whether joyful or challenging, deepen our understanding of existence. When we face our troubles head-on, we uncover a strength far greater than we ever imagined. The Creator is not flawed, and the world is not beyond repair. Healing begins when we tend to our wounds."

Slipping into the bath, she felt the warm water comfort her. Her thoughts drifted to Papa, a dreamer, a writer, a seeker of profound connections within himself and the world. He had wrestled with the loss of Momma, often speaking about the Path of the Soul. "Life feels like a gentle current until a struggle pulls you under," Papa would say. "But with each challenge, having you and Maya beside me lifts me. This journey, guided by the heart, is not easily navigated, but it reveals what truly matters. Challenges and miracles alike shape us, teaching us about life and each other."

Nadia let the warmth soothe her as she reflected on her father's words. The path he described was not a straight line but a winding journey, full of unexpected turns and hidden treasures. It required courage and faith, a willingness to embrace both light and darkness within. In moments of clarity, she felt profound gratitude for the people and experiences that had shaped her. Closing her eyes, she inhaled the calming scent of lavender and whispered a silent prayer of thanks for the strength to keep moving forward.

A pang of longing surfaced as she thought about Maya's struggles. She wished she could ease her sister's pain but recognized that some journeys must be traveled alone. The bath, with its warm embrace, became a refuge where she could reflect and gather strength. Earlier that day, Nadia and Maya had shared a quiet moment in the garden, tending to the trees Momma had planted, staying connected to her and each other.

Nadia replayed Papa's words in her mind, each reflection revealing new layers of meaning. Could she ever fully embody his wisdom and resilience, especially with the uncertainties ahead? After Momma's departure, Papa had found solace in writing short stories. "When we pause to listen, even the smallest treasures have stories to tell," he once said. "A simple seashell, for instance, could hold the whispers of the ocean's music." Nadia marveled at his ability to transform pain into meaningful words, realizing that everyone has the capacity to channel suffering into purpose. In his books, Papa sought a connection with the greater universe.

His voice echoed in her mind, sharing a profound truth: "When a person focuses on their true self, an inner voice guides them, illuminating their path." Tomorrow, Papa would return from Almira, the neighboring town, and Nadia eagerly anticipated his arrival.

Her thoughts shifted to her own experiences, particularly the day Momma's spirit seemed to merge with the sky. Years later, her words still resonated: "Embrace who you are on your journey. Allow yourself to feel, even sorrow, as it takes you to uncharted places. Follow the path of your heart, for it leads to your true self."

Nadia understood the importance of confronting her Momma's passing, a journey that had profoundly shaped her identity. She recognized the universe's rhythms of erosion and rejuvenation, constantly reshaping the energy of creation. Challenges brought renewal, revealing hidden marvels that emerged from hardship, humbling humanity, and instilling a renewed sense of purpose.

Years passed, yet the memory of that fateful day lingered, leaving an enduring ache. Momma's absence was a scar on their hearts. Maya's music echoed through the house, reflecting her melancholic state. After Momma's death, Gabriel helped Maya navigate her grief, but healing was a personal journey. Maya's need for predictability stemmed from a longing for security. Nadia wished Gabriel understood the significance of these routines for Maya.

Nadia's understanding of life's lessons came from her father, whose teachings left an indelible mark. She felt immense gratitude for having such a remarkable parent, the image of her strong, graying-haired father etched in her memory.

Later that night, seeking comfort, Nadia found herself in Maya's room, lying beside her sister. She gently stroked Maya's hair and spoke softly, "Maya, think about the joy Gabriel brings into your life and the future you two can create together. Each new day offers opportunities for positive change. Maybe life is nudging you to explore new possibilities. Gabriel admires your gracefulness, your unwavering kindness, and the light you bring into every room. He sees in you the strength and beauty that sometimes you overlook. Let these gentle whispers of change, and let them guide you. Trust in the journey and in the love, you share, for it is in these connections that we find our true selves."

Nadia lingered for a while, kissing Maya's forehead before retreating to her room. As she lay in bed, her thoughts wandered back to Papa and his imminent return from Almira. The prospect of his presence brought her comfort. She longed to share the news of Gabriel's departure with Papa but hesitated, not wanting to burden him. Instead, Nadia found herself wishing for a spark of excitement to ignite in Maya.

Life's demands for change rarely arrive with kindness or fairness. Instead, they emerged as formidable challenges, bringing waves of pain that tested one's resilience. These changes often felt abrupt and unforgiving, leaving individuals to grapple with their impact. Yet, as time passed, the sharpness of that anguish tended to be dull. Nadia pondered this mysterious contrast—the internal storms of the heart, though fierce and tumultuous, often had the power to cleanse the murky waters of the mind. In the wake of such emotional upheaval, newfound clarity emerged, offering understanding and direction that had previously been obscured.

8

A Nurturing Heart

Hassan, Maya's father, felt the weight of the war settle upon him like a heavy shroud as he walked through Almira, a small town nestled between Zarifa and Daryana. The once-vibrant streets wore the scars of scarcity—empty shelves and rationed supplies whispered tales of hardship and despair. Yet, amid this struggle, a spark of hope ignited within him when he entered Valentina's store. It was a sanctuary, a rare oasis of abundance where he could indulge his beloved daughters. Valentina's shop, nestled in the heart of Almira, was a sensory delight. The tasteful displays, bursting with color, and the enticing aromas of cured meats, aged cheeses, and smoked fish transported visitors to a world of indulgence, a refuge from the surrounding gloom. Hassan admired Valentina's relentless ability to import the finest sausages, cheeses, smoked fish, and pickled vegetables from Russia—a connection forged when she married Izmir during his studies in that distant land. Their conversations often meandered into the enchanting world of the Bolshoi Ballet and the literary treasures of Tolstoy, where Hassan found not just comfort, but a kinship of the mind that transcended the tumult outside.

In this quaint town, where time seemed to slow, Hassan's perspective began to shift. He chose to look beyond the shortages, discovering a newfound appreciation for life's small joys. The comforting scent of freshly baked bread became a balm for his spirit, wrapping him in warm memories of laughter and love. "Amidst all these shortages, we've taken to baking our own bread," he shared with Valentina as he settled his bill, his eyes alight with the warmth of recollection. "The aroma of bread straight from the oven carries me back to my mother's embrace, rekindling my love for its warmth."

As he prepared to leave, Valentina handed him a bag with a playful smile, her eyes twinkling with affection. "I've included some special chocolate truffles for Maya and Nadia. Remember, our home is always open; bring them along next time." Hassan left with a kiss and a heart brimming with gratitude, treasuring these moments and the enduring connection they represented in the midst of chaos.

Retracing his steps to his modest overnight accommodation, darkness wrapped around Almira like a soft, protective blanket. After a refreshing hot shower, he slipped into bed, immersing himself in a book, surrendering to the gentle comfort of sleep.

In the quiet hours before dawn, Hassan stirred uneasily, a fleeting sensation nagging at him, as if the world outside had shifted. Shaking off the unease, he returned to the depths of slumber, clinging to the fleeting comfort of dreams.

Breakfast greeted him with the fragrant allure of Arabic coffee and creamy yogurt, lavishly adorned with walnuts and honey. The spicy, robust notes of the coffee, the tangy yogurt, the crunch of walnuts, and the sweetness of honey danced on his palate—a vibrant symphony of flavors that awakened his senses and fortified his spirit. This satisfying meal was a perfect prelude to the visual feast awaiting him on his homeward journey.

Almira, a village cradled by nature's beauty, unfurled before him like a painter's canvas, each stroke revealing the enchanting charm of this remarkable place. The deserted roads invited him, unveiling houses that dotted the landscape like precious gems scattered amidst flourishing fields. These fields, teeming with vibrant vegetables and golden wheat, celebrated the fertile earth and the devoted hands that tended to it. Hassan couldn't help but marvel at the contrast—the solitude of the roads juxtaposed against the rich, teeming life surrounding him, as if nature itself had chosen this land as its canvas, displaying both fragility and strength.

Serene meadows and pastures cradled the animals of Almira, where goats and cows grazed peacefully, their gentle movements adding to the harmony of the scene. Wild camels roam freely, their untamed beauty a reminder of the wilderness thriving in this corner of the world. A small group of wild goats gathered near a rugged outcrop, their agile movements echoing the resilience of nature, a reflection to survival amid hardship.

Above, a majestic bird soared gracefully, possibly pursuing a fox darting for cover. This aerial dance added a touch of drama to the stunning landscape, a portrayal of the age-old struggle between predators and prey that echoed the human experience.

As Hassan absorbed the beauty of Almira, he felt humbled by its timelessness. In a world where people and civilizations constantly evolved, Almira remained a steadfast reflection of nature's enduring grace. It was a place where the ancient and modern coexisted in seamless harmony, where past and present intertwined, creating a breathtaking canvas of life and resilience.

In that moment, Hassan understood: Almira was not merely a location; it was a living, breathing masterpiece sculpted by time and nature. It reminded him that amid the chaos of an ever-changing world, beauty remained eternal, waiting to be cherished by those fortunate enough to behold it.

Upon his return, Nadia greeted him with a tender kiss, her warmth and joy lifting his spirits. "Two nights away, and look at you… you've become even more beautiful, Nadia," he remarked, the words sparking a joyful thrill in his daughters' hearts, a balm for his own weariness.

"Let me help you with your coat, Papa. Maya's taking a nap," Nadia offered, her voice tinged with concern.

It struck Hassan as unusual for Maya to be in bed on such a glorious, sun-kissed day. Typically, she would abandon everything, rushing to greet him with uncontainable excitement. Sensing something was amiss, he asked, concern lacing his voice, "Is everything alright, Nadia?"

"Nasser left for Paris unexpectedly," Nadia replied, a hint of worry clouding her eyes.

Hassan brushed it off; young people often embarked on adventures, and it didn't particularly trouble him. Yet, his thoughts remained tethered to his daughters, the weight of their emotions drawing him in.

Feeling grateful to be home with Nadia and Maya, he ascended the stairs to Maya's room. He found her somber, her spirits dimmed, as if a shadow had crossed her heart. Wrapping her in his broad embrace, he allowed her tears to flow freely, a release of pent-up emotions.

"I'll miss Nasser," he confessed, understanding the depth of her sorrow as he held her close. "We should grant him some space; a respite from the chaos of war can do wonders. Let's patiently await his call. I'm confident he'll reach out soon."

His soothing words worked their magic on Maya, gradually brightening her thoughts. He gently encouraged her not to dwell on the notion of Nasser meeting other captivating women.

"Even if the women of Paris know more about champagne, ballet, and music, there's nothing we can do about it," he mused, his voice steady and comforting. "If Nasser seeks someone else, he will find her eventually. Now, come—let me brush your hair."

With tender care, he took the hairbrush, his gentle strokes calming her, weaving a sense of peace and reassurance in the quiet room, like a soft lullaby that enveloped them both.

Hassan had been the primary caretaker for his daughters for several years now, a role he embraced with love and dedication. On days like this, the absence of his wife, Nadia, echoed in the corners of his heart, a silent reminder of the love that once filled their home. His love for Nadia was a profound emotion, a connection that transcended the limits of mere words. She was his soulmate, his confidante, and his muse, lighting up his life like a thousand suns, chasing away shadows of loneliness.

Their love was not stagnant; it blossomed with each shared experience, every exchanged smile, and each challenge they faced together. It was a love that evolved, adapting to life's changing seasons while remaining constant in its intensity, a river flowing through the landscape of their lives.

Hassan often found that words fell short when attempting to articulate the depth of his feelings for Nadia. No language could capture the profound emotions she ignited within him. His love was a silent symphony, a masterpiece painted on the canvas of his heart, forever incomprehensible to those who had not known such a love.

In essence, Hassan's love for Nadia was a timeless and boundless force, transcending the limitations of human expression. Even on days when her absence felt like a heavy weight, he cherished that love deeply, for it was a light that guided him through the darkest nights.

As he tenderly ran his fingers through Maya's soft hair, his heart swelled with nostalgia and warmth. The room glowed with the gentle light of midmorning, enveloping them in an atmosphere of serenity and tranquility, a sacred space where love provided refuge from the storms of life.

9

Shadows and Sunshine

Hassan couldn't help but drift into a reverie, recalling the momentous day when Maya had entered their lives. It was a memory etched in his mind like a treasured painting. The day Yasmin, his beloved wife, had shared the news of her pregnancy with him had been a whirlwind of emotions. The sheer excitement and joy that had coursed through him had been unparalleled.

"I don't care whether it's a boy or a girl, Yasmin," he had confessed to her back then, a spark of excitement dancing in his eyes. "I already love our baby." Those words had flowed from the depths of his heart, and as he gazed at Maya now, he understood that his love had only grown stronger with each passing day.

Hassan reflected on the remarkable women who had shaped him into the man he had become. Yasmin, the love of his life and the mother of their precious daughters, had been his steadfast companion through every twist and turn. Her unwavering support and their shared anticipation of their children's arrival had bound them even closer.

In that serene moment, Hassan felt a profound sense of responsibility and wonder. The eagerness he had felt before her birth had transformed into pure joy at being a father. Every milestone, every giggle, and every sweet coo were precious gifts, reminding him of the boundless love he held for his darling girl.

His love for Maya was immeasurable, a boundless wellspring of pride and excitement that filled his heart as he looked at her. He was profoundly grateful for the gift of fatherhood and the love that enveloped their family.

Hassan's mother had been overjoyed upon hearing the news of the impending arrival. He fondly remembered her letters, where she wrote:

"We learn countless lessons from our firstborn, Hassan. No one will teach you more than a baby. They compel you to nurture, to listen, to be patient and kind. They harmonize your heart with the rhythm of the universe. Babies exist outside the confines of time for a while; they will communicate when something doesn't suit them. Life is an extraordinary gift, and you will recognize it the moment you cradle that precious bundle of joy.

Parenthood is an ongoing journey of discovery. Just when I thought I had adapted to having a child, I found myself amazed by a little person who asked questions and rejected vegetables. I barely had time to answer one question before another emerged. That is when I realized how little I truly knew. This is often followed by laughter, tears, tantrums, and tiny feet racing through mud at every opportunity.

They do not merely color within the lines of coloring books; they infuse your world with the vibrant hues of life. They do not require a reason to be joyful. Before you know it, you will be hunting for sequined slippers and ball gowns. Those years of raising you were the most endearing period of my life, and I would not exchange it for anything. Life may be bustling with myriad responsibilities, but children will whisk you away to the carnival and remind you that fun needs no justification. I am immensely proud of you, my son. I am certain you'll be an exceptional father. Just stay away from flutes or drums; their noise might drive you crazy!"

Her letters invariably concluded with a touch of whimsy, and this time it was a mention of her faithful old dog, Betsy. "Although I must admit, even with her allergies, Betsy is easier to manage than children."

Hassan cherished the memory of a time when deciphering the cause of baby Maya's cries felt like an unsolvable riddle. All he could do was scoop her up and hope that his embrace would bring her comfort.

Hassan felt incredibly fortunate to have two such endearing daughters. Nadia, even as a child, had astounded him with her profound discussions about books, poems, and the mysteries of life. Sometimes, he could not help but wonder about her. Her questions, for a child, always delved into intricacies far beyond her tender years. Hassan's response was consistently to procure more books, which Nadia would read and then discuss with him. She would devour as many books as she could, and in her wisdom, she would lovingly wrap them and implore him to send them to a distant orphanage across the world. "These books will ignite the same inspiration in them as they have in me," she declared.

In contrast, Maya found joy in the simple pleasures of wandering, singing, and gathering wildflowers for Yasmin. Music flowed through her veins as effortlessly as the wind rustled through the leaves. To lift her spirits, Hassan suggested with a warm smile, "Maya, my dear, shall we brighten our day? Let's head to the kitchen and prepare a delightful lunch together. Afterwards, how about a leisurely stroll by the lake? The sunshine and refreshing breeze might be just what we need. I'll bring my camera along so we can capture some beautiful moments to share with Nasser."

How many fathers could boast of such an opportunity to spend an afternoon by the lakeside with their cherished daughters? Hassan marveled at the sheer wonder of it all. He vowed, after Yasmin's passing, to savor every precious moment with his daughters as if they were the last. His emotions flowed with childlike simplicity—laughter, kisses, and hugs. Hassan shed tears when overwhelmed with happiness, but he also wept when sadness crept into his heart.

On that particular afternoon, beneath the azure sky, Maya, Nadia, and Hassan reclined on blankets by the lake's shore. Their gazes were drawn to the mirror-like surface of the water, which reflected the lush splendor of the surrounding cedar trees cloaked in autumn hues. Maya reminisced about the day she and Nasser had etched their names onto a tree trunk: "Maya and Nasser, forever." The timeless sounds of nature enveloped them, with the gentle murmur of water and the rustling leaves, unchanged by the passage of time.

As the lake stirred a cascade of memories, Maya glimpsed Nasser's reflection shimmering in the water. Countless summers had seen them paddling across the lake in a canoe or simply basking in the twilight's warmth. The introduction of fish into the lake years ago always brought to mind Hassan's joyous attempt to teach Yasmin how to fish. It brought a soft smile to his lips. The water's reflection danced with the memories of those cherished moments.

In silent admiration, Nadia observed her sister, who had always been her unwavering companion. There was no one she loved more in the world. Despite the radiant day, Nadia noticed the fatigue in Maya's eyes. She reflected, "Whenever misfortune befalls us, it deepens our longing for Momma, compounding our sorrow."

With the upheaval of war, the number of herders and their goats had dwindled. These nomadic herders, in search of lush pastures for their flocks, often paused by the lake, entertaining Hassan and his family with captivating tales of their encounters.

Hassan realized he had forgotten his camera, a fact he shared with his daughters. It seemed like a fortuitous oversight, providing him with a pretext to return to the lake with Maya. Nasser and Maya were foremost in his thoughts. Hassan contemplated, "Love withers under the weight of too many constraints," he mused. "It flourishes when allowed to blossom freely, tender and unconditional. I wish I could offer Maya more comforting words. Disappointments are an inescapable facet of life. We all possess the power to release what burdens us. I want Maya to hold onto her faith in the magnificence of life."

Hassan felt a surge of gratitude towards Nasser, a deep appreciation for the selflessness that had driven him not to involve Maya in his perilous journey. Nasser's unwavering determination and unshakable courage in shouldering this daunting mission alone commanded Hassan's deep respect. Inwardly, Hassan wished he could have shared a heart-to-heart with Nasser, but the complex emotions surrounding this decision weighed on him. Hassan knew that involving Maya in such a venture would have been unbearable for all parties involved, considering the treacherous conditions in Zarifa, which he was unwilling to risk Maya's safety for.

Hassan offered up a silent prayer, a heartfelt plea for Nasser's safe return.

Their hours by the lake had passed without Maya shedding a single tear, yet Nasser's decision had cast a long shadow over her. Doubts about whether she could trust him again lingered in her heart. The fact that Nasser hadn't even cared to inform her gnawed at her core, stoking the fires of anger.

Approaching their home, the comforting scent of Salma's cooking, carried by the breeze mingled with chimney smoke, welcomed them. Salma, Hassan's older sister, had temporarily taken charge of the household during her husband's business trip. She joined them for dinner, her presence offering a reassuring sense of family.

During the meal, Maya found herself unusually reserved, her thoughts seemingly adrift. Nadia attempted to spark a conversation about a new magazine, but Hassan, drained by the day's events, struggled to summon the energy for meaningful engagement. After dinner, he left his daughters chatting with Salma, tenderly kissing each of them goodnight before retreating to his room.

In the quiet solitude of his bedroom, Hassan's thoughts inevitably gravitated towards Yasmin, her absence creating a painful void. Nasser's departure and Maya's sadness made it impossible for Hassan to escape the haunting memories of his late wife and their infant son, Omar.

Hassan had always been a devoted provider, giving Yasmin everything her heart desired. Their life had resembled a fairy tale, a dream brought to life. But everything crumbled when Yasmin departed this world, carrying their unborn son, Omar. That fateful day shattered Hassan's heart, leaving him immobilized. The anguish was suffocating, making each breath a struggle. The thought of life without Yasmin was unthinkable. Were it not for his duty to his young daughters, he might have willingly followed her into the afterlife.

For months, shock and sorrow clung to him like an unrelenting headache, threatening to consume him entirely. Hassan refrained from uttering the word "death," instead allowing Yasmin and baby Omar to remain a gentle presence within his heart. The mere thought of Yasmin drew him deep into the recesses of his soul, where emotions defied explanation. His love for Yasmin, his daughters, and his unborn son had been unwavering. He turned to a higher power, questioning why God had deprived him of love and happiness, concealing his anguish beneath a veneer of strength.

Yasmin's death left an imperishable mark on Hassan's soul, and grief weighed heavily upon him like an invisible cloak he couldn't shake off. It wasn't just her loss that haunted him but the emotional toll it had taken on everyone he cared about.

With the passing months, Hassan found solace in contemplating Divine Wisdom. He vividly recalled moments when he plunged into the depths of his heart to confront the pain. Outwardly, he projected strength, assuring everyone that he was "okay." Yet, the pain gripped him in the unknown corners of his being. He grappled with the unimaginable challenge of carrying on without Yasmin, and the more he contemplated it, the more insurmountable it seemed. At times, he retreated into his thoughts, neglecting his own care. His demeanor mirrored that of a man who had surrendered all hope, and the sight was agonizing to behold.

His office, once bustling with activity, now felt like a ghost town. Paper piled up on his desk, and the phone rarely rang. Hassan sat there, staring blankly at the reports, unable to muster the energy to care. In moments of despair, he even dared to question the very existence of God, feeling abandoned and hopeless.

The smallest things reduced him to tears, the sound of his solitary footsteps during evening walks by the lake, the vacant expanse of his bed. These everyday reminders of his wife were agonizing, and the sadness smoldered within him, unrelenting, much like the unwavering glow of a lamp. Sometimes, grief and sadness enshrouded him like a clinging mist. On days when comprehending the magnitude of his loss proved impossible, he quietly reminded himself, "I must keep walking and breathing until I'm once again immersed in the world." Each gentle caress of sunlight upon his face assured him that another world existed beyond the veil of grief. To dispel the dense fog within, he learned to let his sorrow drift away like a breeze, clearing the way for vitality and affection to arrive. His love for Yasmin, Nadia, Maya, and Omar served as a lifeline, calling him back from the abyss. The sense of belonging and being rooted somewhere bestowed upon him the strength to endure.

The house had taken on an air of desolation, like the hillside graveyard. A year had passed since Yasmin's departure when Salma, assuming responsibility for Hassan's household, suggested a reprieve. "It's time, Hassan," she insisted, her eyes gleaming with a mixture of determination and love. "You need to visit our younger sister, Saira, in Switzerland. The lakes are frozen, and it's the perfect opportunity for the girls to learn to ski. Plus, who could resist hot chocolate in a snowy wonderland?"

Hassan chuckled softly, imagining his daughters bundled up in ski gear. "And perhaps I can learn how to stand on two sticks without falling flat on my face," he replied with a faint smile.

Salma fondly reminisced about her last visit to a village nestled deep within the Swiss Alps, a place so picturesque it felt like it had been plucked straight from a postcard. This haven, adorned in a pristine blanket of snow, embodied the essence of a winter wonderland, drawing travelers from across the globe. Its charm emanated from cobblestone streets winding through the village and towering, snow-capped peaks forming a majestic backdrop. With winter's arrival, a transformative magic enveloped the region. The serene lakes that adorned the landscape froze over, becoming expansive, glistening sheets of ice. These frozen waters, surrounded by snow-covered hills, became the canvas for myriad winter activities that captivated both villagers and visitors alike.

Throughout the winter months, the village thrived with activity. Both locals and tourists eagerly embraced the season, finding joy in the frozen lakes and abundant opportunities for outdoor adventures.

Despite the sub-zero temperatures, the village exuded warmth and camaraderie. Streetlamps adorned with twinkling lights illuminated the snowy pathways, guiding the way through wintry streets. Laughter and the melodious clinking of glass filled the crisp mountain air, painting a vivid picture of shared moments and cherished memories. In Salma's recollection, this Swiss village remained eternally carved as a sanctuary of natural beauty and communal spirit, inviting all to experience the enchantment of its winter embrace.

Hassan fondly remembered how Hans, Saira's Swiss husband, graciously opened his home and heart to them. "You'll love it here!" he exclaimed, his infectious enthusiasm lighting up the room. Hans, temporarily setting aside his demanding medical practice, devoted himself to bringing laughter and joy to Hassan's daughters on the ice. The girls persistently urged, "Come, Papa, join us!" Maya and Nadia's laughter echoed across the ice as they raced each other, their cheeks flushed from the cold and excitement. For a moment, Hassan allowed himself to laugh with them, feeling a flicker of warmth in his heart. With reluctance, he finally succumbed to their pleas, emerging from his self-imposed isolation.

The warmth of crackling fires, Saira's exquisite culinary creations, and the joy of teaching Maya and Nadia how to ski breathed life back into Hassan's once desolate spirit. As he skated, danced, and played with his daughters on the frozen lake, he was reminded of a profound truth he had once read: music resides within every person. On the ice, he heard that music again, and the dormant child within him reawakened, leaping, dancing, and occasionally stumbling in playful abandon. All it had taken was a chance to frolic.

During those weeks, it felt as though he had been locked in a prolonged emotional slumber. Little did he realize that numerous facets of his inner self had remained dormant, patiently awaiting the opportunity to reawaken.

Hassan believed their time away marked a pivotal juncture in Maya and Nadia's journey towards accepting Yasmin's passing. After a few days, the girls lay in the snow, creating snow angels while whispering, "This is for you, Mama and baby Omar, goodnight." Their innocence and sincerity made Hassan's heart swell, reminding him that love persists even in the absence.

He and Hans reclined by the warm, crackling fireplace, sipping wine and engaging in deep, heartfelt conversation. Their shared passion for literature and poetry sparked a profound connection. "You know," Hans mused, "poetry is like a window into the soul. It reveals what lies beneath the surface." Hassan nodded in agreement, appreciating how these words resonated with his own experiences. Both Hassan and Hans held a deep reverence for the eloquent language of the soul, beautifully portrayed by poets. These poets, in their relentless exploration of human suffering, the longing for love, life's challenges, and unexpected, life-altering events, crafted powerful and moving verses that resonated deeply with Hassan and Hans. To these poets, the transient nature of what held sway in a person's life served as a reminder that, through candid and unfiltered introspection, one could forge a richer connection with life.

Much like the captivating melodies of music, poetry had the power to rekindle the childlike wonder within Hassan's heart. Through his own ventures into crafting verses, he discovered that embracing life's experiences was the first step toward learning to coexist with them.

The six weeks spent with Hans and Saira flew by in blissful abandon. Now, it was time to return home, yet Hassan couldn't help but wish these days of rejuvenation would stretch on indefinitely. His yearning for Yasmin remained a constant ache, and the thought of having found the strength to move on filled him with trepidation. All he could do was remain true to his emotions.

On that final night away, the absence of Yasmin and Omar weighed heavily on Hassan's heart. The bright stars scattered across the inky night sky beckoned him to look up. Adjusting his gaze, he sought to capture a whisper from the heavens. His head tilted with a hint of sorrow. "Look, I am here," he murmured to the night sky, convinced that Yasmin had secured God's permission to watch over him. The tender voices within his heart continually reaffirmed this belief.

Returning indoors, he found Hans tending to the fire, its warmth rekindling his dormant spirit. As Hassan sat by the fire, lost in his thoughts, he heard the laughter of his daughters pulling him back to the present.

Saira entered, bearing a tray laden with hot chocolate and ginger biscuits. Gratitude swelled within Hassan for the presence of this remarkable and beautiful sister in his life.

As Hassan lay in bed, thoughts of that trip from years ago resurfaced, stirring restlessly in his mind. Over the years, he had learned to let go of the past by closing his eyes and embarking on a fresh start. He thought of his lovely daughter, Maya, whose striking resemblance to Yasmin served as a constant reminder. "I'm certain Yasmin knows just how proud I am of her," Hassan mused. Even now, it was impossible for him to contemplate anything other than how precious Maya was to him.

Yasmin had always been meticulous in her teachings, ensuring that the girls adhered to a disciplined schedule. She had never harbored any resentment towards Hassan, and he had pledged to care for her beloved girls, shielding them from the harsh realities of the world. He had embarked on a journey to help them understand that life was indeed beautiful, even in the face of adversity.

10

Love in the Distances

Stepping out of the airport, Nasser was immediately captivated by Paris's distinctive charm. His cab ride to the hotel felt like a scenic tour through the heart of the city. He gazed in awe at the Louvre Museum, the elegant bridges over the Seine River, and bustling cafes alive with Parisians and visitors savoring rich espresso.

Upon arriving at his hotel, Nasser received a warm welcome from the concierge, whose soft French tones made him feel instantly at home. The hotel exuded charm, tastefully decorated and bathed in the gentle Parisian light streaming through large windows.

As Nasser settled into his new surroundings, he couldn't help but feel swept away by the realization that he was embarking on a thrilling new chapter in his life. Standing by the window, he gazed out at the delightful Parisian streets below, where people moved to the rhythm of their daily lives. The city's architecture seamlessly melded historic grandeur with modern elegance.

Later that evening, Nasser ventured out for a quick snack. The streets were alive with the melodic cadence of French conversations and the tantalizing aroma of freshly baked bread. He paused to admire a small boulangerie, the golden croissants glistening under the warm lights. As evening descended and the lights of Paris began to twinkle like stars, his heart swelled with wonder and gratitude for the incredible opportunity that lay before him.

Yet, even as Nasser immersed himself in the city's mesmerizing beauty, his heart ached for Maya. The Eiffel Tower's elegance and the Seine River's poetic charm couldn't fill the void left by her absence. He called her faithfully every day, a lifeline to the love he cherished. Each time Maya's name appeared on his phone, his heart skipped a beat, hoping to hear her voice. But the silence continued, and his longing grew stronger.

"What if she never answers?" he confided in Hassan during a video call. "I can't keep doing this without her."

"You must let her know you're there, even from afar," Hassan advised, leaning back in his chair, his gaze thoughtful. "Sometimes, love is about patience and understanding. The world is vast, but love can bridge any distance."

Through Hassan's comforting words, Nasser found solace. Yet, he understood that the silence from Maya was not just an absence; it was a growing tension, an uncharted territory that made him question everything. He felt like a ship caught between the vibrant life of Paris and the quiet waters of his longing.

In moments of reflection, Nasser often found himself at the window, gazing out at the bustling Parisian streets. Despite the city's captivating backdrop, it seemed a world away from the tranquility of their shared moments by the lake.

In his heart, Hassan held a sacred place, a figure deserving of deep respect and admiration. To Nasser, Hassan was more than just Maya's father; he was a source of wisdom and unwavering support.

Through Hassan's understanding gaze, Nasser found hope in the swirling chaos of his emotions. Their conversations lingered in his thoughts long after they ended, each word a tribute to the profound impact of their relationship. In those moments, Nasser began to realize that Hassan represented everything he yearned for—love, empathy, and steadfast support.

But as the days turned into weeks, Nasser knew he couldn't remain trapped in the solitude of his longing. He had to embrace the beauty around him, even as he cherished the memories of his love for Maya. With each passing day in Paris, he vowed to honor their connection, not just through silence, but through every experience he would share with the city—a promise to keep their love alive amidst the vibrant pulse of life.

In the midst of it all, Maya's heart was a stormy sea, its emotions crashing against the shores of her soul with relentless intensity. Each day seemed to usher in a new tempest, swirling with conflicting emotions that threatened to pull her under.

She wished she were like other women who seemed so much more capable, stronger, and more ambitious than she felt. It left her feeling like she was stumbling through each day, barely keeping up. She felt overshadowed by women who shone with brilliance.

Confusion reigned in the maze of her thoughts and feelings. It was as though she was trapped in a labyrinth, with every twist and turn leading to more uncertainty. She wrestled with the whirlpool of emotions, struggling to find a way through the conflicting currents surging through her heart.

Sometimes, her heart felt like a torrential downpour of sorrow, an unending rain that soaked her in grief. She stood by the window, watching the rain, her shoulders shaking with silent sobs as the memories of Nasser's embrace haunted her. She longed for Nasser's presence, yearning for the warmth of his embrace and the reassurance of his love. The pain of his absence cut deep, leaving wounds that seemed impossible to heal.

Yet, amidst the tempest, there were moments of longing and desire, like rays of sunlight breaking through dark clouds. She cherished the sweet memories of their time together—stolen glances, whispered words of affection. These moments of warmth and tenderness were precious rays of hope that pierced through the storm clouds, reminding her of the deep love she held for Nasser.

However, there were also moments when anger and frustration surged within her like lightning bolts illuminating the dark sky. She struggled to understand why Nasser had chosen to leave, why he had embarked on this path of separation. These emotions clashed with her deep love for him, creating an inner conflict that tore at her very soul. "Why did you leave, Nasser? What am I supposed to do with all this love now?" she thought, her mind a storm of unanswered questions.

In the midst of this emotional tempest, Maya sought refuge in solitude. She withdrew from the world, seeking solace in the quiet corners of her mind. The smell of rain-soaked earth mingled with her tears, grounding her sorrow in the present moment. Through introspection, she attempted to untangle the web of thoughts and emotions that constantly tugged at her heart. She yearned for clarity and understanding, a way to navigate the storm within.

Despite the turmoil raging inside her, Maya's heart remained resilient. It was a reflection of the enduring power of love—a love that refused to be extinguished by the storms of life. Deep within, she clung to the hope that someday, the tempest would subside, and the waters of her heart would find peace. Until then, she bravely navigated the turbulent seas, knowing that amidst the chaos, there was a love that would endure, no matter the challenges it faced. Her love for Nasser was a flame that burned brightly, casting a warm glow even in the darkest of times.

Nadia stared at her distraught sister, Maya, her heart heavy with the desire to offer comfort, yet she found herself at a loss for words. As she observed Maya's troubled expression, Nadia couldn't help but wonder what was going on in her sister's mind. She imagined that Maya's thoughts were likely a swirling storm of confusion and pain, but at that moment, there seemed to be nothing she could say to ease her sister's suffering.

"Do you want to talk about it?" Nadia finally asked, her voice gentle yet uncertain.

Maya shook her head, her eyes glistening with unshed tears. "I don't know what to say, Nadia. It's like everything inside me is a tangled mess."

Nadia reached out, her fingers trembling as they found Maya's, a silent promise of unwavering support. "I'm here for you, no matter what," she said softly.

Nadia's mind began to wander, contemplating the futility of it all. She thought about how, ironically, she felt a sense of helplessness mirroring that of Nasser, who often struggled to find the right words to express himself. Nadia realized that sometimes, in the face of someone's deep emotional turmoil, words could feel inadequate, like fragile bridges over a vast abyss of pain.

Despite her inability to articulate her feelings to Maya, Nadia's heart ached with empathy. She hoped that, in that silent moment of shared understanding, her sister could find solace knowing she was not alone in her suffering.

In quiet moments of reflection, Nadia realized that happiness wasn't about reaching milestones or meeting others' expectations. It was about understanding herself, listening to her heart, and showing herself kindness. Watching Maya struggle, Nadia recognized how challenging it was for her to navigate life's ever-changing landscape. Strength and courage were qualities Maya needed to uncover within herself, and peace would come through accepting things as they were.

11

Between Fragments and Silence

As Nasser navigated the whirlwind of his new life in Paris, the city hummed around him, alive with energy and possibility. "This place is amazing," he confided to a friend during a brief rendezvous at a café, though a bittersweet ache lingered in his heart, calling back to the simplicity of Daryana.

"Have you heard from Maya?" his friend asked, concern etching lines of worry on their face.

Nasser let out a sigh, frustration bubbling just beneath the surface. "No, she won't answer my calls. I just wish she could understand... I never meant to hurt her." He fiddled with his coffee cup, the warmth a stark contrast to the chill in his heart.

His friend nodded, his empathy palpable. "It's tough. But maybe giving her space would help? She needs time to process her feelings."

Meanwhile, Maya was lost in her own tempest of emotions, finding solace only in the embrace of her violin. "Why does this feel so impossible?" she murmured to herself, her fingers gliding over the strings, the familiar notes filling the room with echoes of bittersweet memories. Each note resonated like a plea, stirring up emotions she wished she could silence.

"Maya, you have to talk to him," Hassan urged one evening as he watched her play, the weight of their shared history heavy in the air. "He's hurting, and so are you. It doesn't have to be like this."

"I just... I can't," Maya whispered, tears shimmering in her eyes. "What if I'm not enough for him?" She put down her violin, the silence in the room amplifying her doubts.

Hassan paused, his gaze steady and reassuring. "You are everything to him, Maya. You hold the power to shape this story however you wish." He leaned in, his voice dropping to a softer tone. "Remember the way you two laughed together? How your music seemed to create its own world? That connection is real."

Yet, amidst his concern for Maya, Hassan felt a flicker of impatience, perhaps fueled by the weight of his own demanding schedule. He wished she wouldn't harbor anger toward him.

To Nasser, the hospital felt like a place where profits eclipsed people, and he yearned for a life that transcended work. He carried with him the lessons imparted by his parents—reminders of the importance of family and the unwavering support that had been his anchor throughout life's tempests. He often thought about how his mother would sit with him during tough times, her hand on his shoulder, reminding him of the love that surrounded him.

Despite the turbulence surrounding him, Nasser resolved to give Paris—and his relationship with Maya—the time they both needed. He sought a delicate balance between career and personal life, determined never to lose sight of what truly mattered.

Then, as if guided by fate, he stumbled upon a furnished apartment just a stone's throw from the local hospital. It felt serendipitous, a source of hope in his search for a place to call home. This apartment promised not just convenience but also a sense of comfort that wrapped around him like a soothing retreat.

Nestled in a quaint, tree-lined neighborhood, the building radiated a welcoming charm. Its brick façade and well-tended garden hinted at a community rich in pride and camaraderie. As Nasser stepped into the lobby, friendly neighbors greeted him with genuine smiles, welcoming him into this new chapter.

Inside, the apartment was a true gem. The moment Nasser crossed the threshold, he was enveloped by an inviting ambiance. The living room, adorned with tasteful furnishings, invited him with a plush sofa and cozy armchairs arranged around a coffee table, all bathed in soft, natural light spilling through large windows. The décor blended modernity with comfort, creating a tranquil sanctuary.

The bedroom was equally inviting—a queen-sized bed draped in soft luxurious linens awaited him. A spacious walk-in closet offered ample room for his belongings.

Being within walking distance of the medical facility brought Nasser tremendous relief. The ease of access to work spared him the burden of long commutes. As the sun dipped below the horizon on his first day in the apartment, Nasser felt a profound sense of contentment wash over him. He had not merely found a place to live but a true sanctuary where he could begin to rebuild his life.

He longed to share the news of his new apartment with Maya, hoping it might serve as a bridge across the widening gap between them. Yet, Maya remained distant, refusing to speak with him, leaving Nasser with a sense of disappointment that settled like a stone in his heart.

In his frustration, Nasser turned to Hassan, who was a steadfast source of enthusiasm and encouragement. Hassan had a remarkable ability to infuse hope into Nasser's life, illuminating the shadows of uncertainty that clung to him.

As they discussed the details of his new apartment, Nasser felt a deep sense of gratitude for Hassan's friendship. Their conversations were like lifelines, assurances that amidst life's difficulties, there were still people who cared deeply and stood by him through thick and thin.

"I wish it was safe for you to invite her over to see the apartment?" said Hassan sadly. It would have been nice to show her that you're building a life there.

Despite the challenges with Maya, Nasser held fast to hope—that, with time and patience, she might find it in her heart to reconnect with him. He understood that mending their relationship would require effort from both sides, but he was willing to wait, to nurture the bond they had once shared.

Meanwhile, Hassan couldn't shake his concern for Maya as the days slipped by, her silence growing heavier. She stubbornly continued to decline Nasser's calls, immersing herself in her music, the only refuge that brought her solace. In those moments of longing for Nasser or missing her mother, she poured her heart into her violin, letting the melodies carry her emotions. One evening, as she played a haunting tune, memories flooded her mind—laughter shared over coffee, late-night jam sessions, and the warmth of Nasser's presence.

Hassan often found himself reminiscing about the times when Maya and Nasser played music together, their harmonious blend of violin and guitar creating melodies that resonated from deep within their souls. The joy and beauty of their collaboration felt almost magical, and Hassan imagined that each note they shared had evoked powerful emotions, an unspoken connection woven through their music.

As he sat in the quiet of the evening, bathed in the warm glow of the setting sun, Hassan could no longer contain his concern. "Maya," he began gently, his voice tinged with sadness, "you deserve more than this. Nasser has been reaching out, and he's hurting without you. But what matters most is how you feel."

Hassan understood that embracing change could be a difficult journey, filled with uncertainty and conflicting thoughts. Yet he recognized that Maya needed to make a decision that would lead her to inner peace.

With compassion, he encouraged her to prioritize her own feelings above all else. "Consider forgiving Nasser, if you can," he suggested softly. "You have the power to rewrite your own story, and I'll be here to support you in whatever choice you make."

"Maya," Papa observed, "Nasser has always brought laughter and joy into your life. I've seen the unique connection you share, and it's clear he loves you deeply."

Maya looked at her father, appreciating his wisdom and sincerity. Yet, despite his comforting words, doubts still swirled in her mind. Just as Nasser wrestled with the temptation to leave, she couldn't bear the thought of being second place in his life. Still, she felt the gentle pull of her father's guidance deep within her.

With curiosity flickering in her heart, Maya asked, "How can you be so certain, Papa?"

With unwavering conviction, Papa replied, "I have never been more certain about anything in my life. Sometimes, the truth is a matter of how we choose to perceive it."

And indeed, the truth remained clear: Nasser had always centered his life around Maya. This was not mere exaggeration; she meant everything to him. It would pain him deeply to know that his brief deviation had cast shadows of doubt in her heart.

In his final words, Papa concluded, "What you and Nasser share is undeniably real, Maya."

12

Beneath The Rising Sun

Maya awoke with the first light of dawn, the horizon painted in tender hues of gold and pink. The soft murmur of Hassan and Nadia's dreams floated through the air, cocooning her in the tranquil softness of early morning. She smiled, tiptoeing past them, a delicate wicker basket in hand.

"Where are you off to?" Hassan's sleepy voice broke the stillness.

"Just for a little walk by the lake," she replied, her heart fluttering with the promise of the day.

"Don't forget to bring back something for breakfast!" Nadia called, her voice thick with sleep.

With a gentle nod, Maya embarked on her pilgrimage toward the serene lakeshore. Inside her basket nestled a cherished blanket, a flask brimming with aromatic Arabic coffee, and a platter adorned with freshly sliced, glistening fruits. Each step toward the water felt charged with magic, the air pulsing with possibility. She inhaled deeply, letting the scents of dew and earth wrap around her.

As she walked, memories flickered in her mind like fleeting shadows—performing with an orchestra, standing before an audience lost in the music. Those dreams felt distant now, like echoes fading in the morning mist.

The sunrise began painting delicate brushstrokes across the sky, the world glowing with the gentle radiance of dawn. Maya spread her blanket on the dew-kissed earth, preparing for the celestial spectacle. She closed her eyes, letting the morning breeze caress her face. A shadow of longing lingered, but she pushed it aside. "Focus, Maya. This is a moment for you," she whispered to herself.

The immense sphere of celestial fire, radiant in shades of orange and gold, timidly emerged from below the horizon, announcing its grand entrance. In that poignant moment, a wave of continuity washed over her. "Love," she mused, her heart swelling, "is a vital force that nurtures and supports life, always delicately balanced."

As she poured herself a steaming cup of coffee, her gaze fixated on the graceful ospreys gliding over the water, searching for their morning meal. With the coffee cup cradled in her hands, she savored the aroma, inhaling deeply as the soft breeze rustled through the leaves. "I wonder if the herd boys will be out today," she thought, picturing their laughter as they ascended the nearby hills.

Maya had intentionally steered clear of certain thoughts, but the growing void left by Nasser's absence crept back in. "That was a mistake," she murmured, the weight of her realization pressing down on her. "I need to make changes."

"Why do you think he calls?" Nadia's voice echoed in her mind, a question that had lingered in the air between them.

The truth felt heavier. Nasser had been her sanctuary, the gentle balm for the ache left by her mother's absence. Deep inside, a little girl still sat on her bed, lost in the shadows of grief, quietly longing for comfort. "Pain," she reflected, "is like a storm cloud gathering strength, circling within until it feels too heavy to bear."

In that moment, Maya reached out to that inner child, wrapping her in warmth and safety. "You're not alone," she whispered, a promise in her heart. The thought of life without Nasser loomed large, casting a shadow over her. He was the only man who had truly understood her, yet he was miles away in a city that felt like a distant dream.

"Have I betrayed my heart?" she murmured, her voice trembling with uncertainty. In her mind, images of a joyful reunion with Nasser flickered like candles in the dark. She could see the warmth of his smile, feel the soft brush of his fingertips against her skin, and imagine their souls intertwining. Yet beneath that sweet longing lay a deep ache, a poignant reminder of the struggles that had led her to this crossroads.

Today felt different. "I have to reach out," she decided, a gentle nudge within urging her forward. Maya pictured Nasser's face lighting up with joy at her call. "Maybe we can talk about everything," she thought, the anticipation warming her heart.

As she reflected, Maya was struck by how easily those cherished memories surfaced, each a tribute to a connection that felt utterly irreplaceable. Today, she found a strange comfort in the rhythm of his daily calls—Nasser was persistent, calling her each day, and when she didn't pick up, he'd reach out to Hassan or Nadia. But today, that bond felt like a thread stretching thin, the distance between them becoming palpable.

Maya and Nadia lived vibrant lives— dinners at lively restaurants, nights lost in the enchanting haze of shisha lounges, and evenings of carefree dancing. Yet, amidst all this joy, Maya wrestled with an unshakeable yearning for something deeper, a solace that eluded her grasp. The thought of sharing her struggles with Nasser felt daunting, the raw honesty of her emotions tangled with her own imperfections.

"This is my life," she whispered aloud, the sound almost foreign. "Rich with love, steeped in beauty, tinged with sorrow." The sudden loss of Yasmin had shaken her to her core, casting her into a vast sea of emptiness.

"I haven't been my best self," she admitted, her voice barely above a whisper. In her pursuit of love, she began to see how her narrow perspective had tinted her relationships. "Nasser has his burdens," she thought. "It's time to loosen my grip on judgment."

"It's unfortunate that my selfish desire to possess him has shaped my view of his choices," she continued, the weight of her thoughts shifting. "I have no right to expect him to sacrifice his own needs for me." She paused, feeling a swell of resolve. "In a relationship like this, one truth remains—it's bound to wither if not nurtured. I yearn for freedom, even as I stand at the crossroads, uncertain of the way forward. But I must lay my heart bare beneath the open sky."

As she contemplated Nasser's tender spirit, a wave of astonishment washed over her. How close she had come to squandering the opportunity to be with someone so rare! Standing at the edge of the lake, she gazed into the shimmering water, feeling a renewed sense of purpose wash over her. "I can't lose this," she vowed, carefully folding her blanket and setting her course homeward.

When she reached the house, Hassan looked up, his face illuminating at the sight of her. "You look radiant, Maya!" he exclaimed, his smile bursting like sunlight breaking through clouds. He leaned in and pressed a warm kiss on her cheek, a simple gesture that filled her with warmth and hope.

"Thanks, Papa. I was thinking of making pancakes for breakfast," she replied, her heart fluttering with the warmth of his affection.

Hassan chuckled, a twinkle in his eye. "I'd love that, but I have a pressing appointment to get to. Save some for me, will you? I'll be back to savor those pancakes later."

As he hurried out, Maya felt a wave of reassurance wash over her. In that moment, she knew everything would be alright for her, a quiet certainty settling in her heart.

Maya approached the grand piano with gentle grace, her fingers hovering over the keys. She closed her eyes, letting the soft, melodic tune fill the air, each note a balm for her soul. In that moment, music became her sanctuary, a refuge that transported her deep into the well of her emotions. "I didn't realize how much I needed this," she whispered.

With a heart overflowing with gratitude, she silently acknowledged the divine intervention that had created distance between her and Nasser. It was the only balm strong enough to soothe the storm within her.

As the notes cascaded around her, an epiphany blossomed. "I am both my own best friend and my own worst enemy," she mused. "Love is like a brilliant star in the darkest of nights, requiring relentless effort to keep my head held high. I must keep reaching for those stars."

Maya glided her fingers across the piano keys, her mind drifting. "No matter how brightly the sun shines, the sky makes no promises. We are mirrors of its unpredictability. Life, in its raw, untamed beauty, touches us in ways we never expect, leaving its mark with each shift and turn."

Recognizing the complexities of her life, she acknowledged the fear bubbling beneath the surface. "Perhaps we are always in flux, drawn to the beauty within life's mysteries, like bees captivated by blossoms on their sacred journey."

As she played, each note spoke a deep truth—a message that love, strength, and the search for ourselves are all connected in our journey. Maya's path had been long and winding, peppered with joy and sorrow, clarity and confusion. Yet, in the soft morning light, she caught a glimmer of hope. Her love for Nasser would always be part of her, but now it was time to embrace her own strength.

Love, in all its forms, was a journey of continuous growth and transformation. With this realization, she felt ready to confront whatever challenges lay ahead, knowing that her heart's compass would always point her true north

13

Beneath the City's Shadows

It was pure chance that drew Nasser's attention to a conversation unfolding on the bustling Parisian sidewalk. Two women were engaged in an animated discussion, their voices carrying a curious accent that piqued Nasser's curiosity. He watched as one of the women gratefully accepted a small sum of money from the other. It was an ordinary scene in a city filled with strangers, but something about it held his gaze.

Normally, Nasser wasn't one to strike up conversations with unfamiliar faces. He suspected, as many did in such instances, that the woman might be begging for spare change. Yet, an inexplicable impulse welled up within him. He couldn't resist extending a helping hand.

With a moment's pause, he turned his attention fully to the slender, delicate figure before him. He cleared his throat and ventured, "Are you from Zarifa?"

The woman's eyes widened in surprise, her response barely more than a shy and soft-spoken "Yes."

Nasser found himself taken aback by the unexpected connection. He handed her a generous note and said, "I hope this helps, even if it's just a little." The woman nodded gratefully, her eyes filled with unspoken gratitude. Nasser gave a small smile and continued on his way to work, his thoughts lingering on the brief exchange.

As he navigated the bustling streets, Nasser couldn't help but reflect on the state of the world. Technology had advanced by leaps and bounds, yet humanity and common decency seemed to have been left behind. The world he mused, was filled with people driven by greed, yearning to dominate others. They masked their intentions with lofty words like "peace" while sowing terror, division, and chaos.

Nasser's thoughts deepened as he considered the cunning tactics employed by those who sought to control the world. They portrayed their own nations as architects of civilization, casting the rest of the world as rough, congested, and uncivilized. They invented intricate narratives to convince everyone that certain countries posed a grave threat to world order.

In the heart of the bustling metropolis, Nasser felt the weight of these injustices. As he continued his journey to work, he couldn't shake the belief that the world needed more than just technological progress—it needed a resurgence of humanity, compassion, and genuine decency.

That evening, as Nasser was on his way back to his flat, he caught sight of one of the women again. Even in the dimming light, her hair and well-worn clothes gave her an air of dignity. There was no trace of greed or desperation about her. What was it that compelled him to approach her? Was it a fleeting moment of madness or the pulsing of his own heart? Despite their apparent differences, Nasser felt an inexplicable pull towards this woman. An unspoken curiosity welled up within him, urging him to learn more about her. Her skin was flawless, her hands delicate, and her manners impeccable. In an odd way, she reminded him of his mother.

As Nasser strolled past with his slicked-back black hair and stylish designer attire, some onlookers couldn't help but wonder about his interest in the woman. Others merely cast them a begrudging glance. Then, a tall and elegantly dressed man nonchalantly tossed a coin in her direction.

Nasser couldn't help but reflect on the many people he had seen on the streets who exuded elegance and success. Yet, if you looked into their eyes, you could discern something different—a cold, distant, and unmistakably unhappy gaze. It was a revelation that struck him like a bolt of lightning. He realized that deep down, we are all tethered by some form of suffering and pain. Misery had the power to cast a shadow even in the brightest corners of paradise.

"How have I wronged anyone?" the woman asked, her voice tinged with sadness. "My husband worked tirelessly to secure a comfortable life for us. We were ultimately forced to flee Zarifa with a few friends on the night, our homes and lives were destroyed. My husband, fluent in French, believed he could find work here in Paris. I pretended not to see the worry in his eyes. He was always concerned and protective of me.

"At fifty-eight years old, he suffered a heart attack just a few days after our arrival, and I used most of our savings to try and save him. Tragically, he passed away. I am grateful that he did not leave this world alone. I often look around and wonder how many unknown, sad souls depart from this earth each day, unnoticed.

"Perhaps that will become my fate, for I am alone now. I once feared losing everything, but then I grew afraid of having nothing. I fear now that nothing lasts forever, no matter how carefully we protect it. I couldn't find work, and I was too ashamed to beg on the streets. I spent many hours pondering how I've always followed the rules, how I've tried my best to make the world a better place. Consumed by sadness and despair for days, yet death did not come to rescue me.

"I embrace the truth that there is no shame in having nothing. This stark reality has been forced upon me by the ravages of war, but I steadfastly refuse to let it define who I am. I have endured countless nights alone, my heart holding onto hope for brighter tomorrows, my mind envisioning dreams of self-sufficiency."

Together with a few souls from Zarifa, I have found refuge in an aging townhouse. In the face of scarcity, we have turned discarded potato skins into thriving plants and rescued vegetables from nearby shops, creating a lush garden around our humble home.

Every evening, as we gather for a meal, a prayer of gratitude escapes our lips, thanking God that our stomachs are not empty. Our once gloomy dwelling now radiates warmth and cheer, adorned with the vibrant colors of our new garden. In these simple, often overlooked things, we find deep solace. It is in these moments that I dare to dream — of nurturing a harvest large enough to feed not only ourselves but also the hungry souls wandering our streets, craving a bit of kindness and warmth.

"Did you know that if all the homeless hearts in the world were to unite, we could forge our own nation?" she continued. "We could create a sanctuary built on compassion, understanding, and love. These dreams, inspired by my husband's memory, fill my spirit with vitality. He, too, believed in the power of kindness — in the limitless impact of a single, selfless gesture. Through these acts, hope is ignited, flickering like a light in the darkest of nights. They remind us all that even in the most challenging circumstances, humanity's inherent goodness can light the way toward a better, more compassionate world."

This wise woman had a remarkable way of touching his heart. He wished he could do more for her, but time was not on his side. As he handed her some money and continued on his way, his thoughts turned to the issue of landlords. It had become a troubling trend for them to occupy poorly maintained buildings that housed desperate and suffering tenants. The plumbing, elevator, and electrical wiring were predictably old and unreliable, and the paint had long since faded.

"It's as if people aren't suffering enough," Nasser thought angrily. He reflected on how tenants were often packed into these condemned spaces solely for the profit of landlords. "There are people out there protesting about the price of healthcare. How many people think about the homeless?"

As Nasser made his way back to his flat, his thoughts inevitably turned to Maya. He missed gazing into her deep eyes and caressing her exquisite face. Her lustrous hair, wit, and charming personality had left an inerasable mark on his heart.

Maya's charm and enchanting music always brought Nasser immense joy. He couldn't help but wonder, "How much longer, Maya? How much longer will you keep your distance from me?" He had resolved to wait patiently, for as long as it took, until she gave him a sign. Days turned into weeks, and all his waking hours were spent loving her from afar.

It felt as though they had become like distant stars, separated by an unbridgeable cosmic expanse. Maya, once so close, now seemed light-years away, and Nasser found himself adrift in uncertainty. He longed for any glimmer of hope, a flicker of recognition from her, because his days had become an endless stream of devotion and longing.

As he gazed up at the night sky, he couldn't help but draw a parallel between their situation and the stars that punctuated the darkness above him. Distant, yet radiant, they held secrets and mysteries just like Maya. Nasser remained resolute, ready to traverse the vastness of the universe if that's what it took to reach her.

As the evening sun cast a warm glow over the city, Maya finally found the courage to forgive Nasser. Her heart, burdened by the weight of their estrangement, began to lighten with each passing moment. The decision to call him was not made lightly; it was a choice she had pondered for days.

As she dialed his number, her fingers trembled with a mix of anticipation and nervousness. The phone rang, and with each passing ring, her heart raced faster. Then, a familiar voice answered on the other end, and it was as if a floodgate of emotions burst open within her.

"Hello, Nasser," she said, her voice quivering with a blend of vulnerability and excitement. Just hearing his name brought a rush of memories, both sweet and painful, back to the surface.

14

Love Across Distances

Nasser felt a flutter of excitement in his chest as he lifted the phone, his palms slightly damp with anticipation. When Maya's voice spilled through the receiver, it was like a cherished song—sweet and soothing, filling the empty spaces in his heart that had echoed with silence for far too long.

"Nasser?" Her voice trembled with a blend of hope and disbelief, and it made his breath catch.

"Yes, it's me." He steadied himself, trying to infuse his tone with calmness. Her warm, gentle laughter wrapped around him like a tender embrace, rekindling a warmth he had thought was lost forever.

Their conversation flowed effortlessly, like a river winding through their shared past and present. They chatted about the mundane—the weather, the empty shelves left in the wake of the war in Zarifa, and friends whose faces they missed—but every word resonated with deeper significance, layered with unspoken emotions and cherished memories. Each exchange was not merely a recounting of facts; it was a dance of connection, a reminder of everything that had once brought them together and everything that still lingered between them.

"I didn't realize I could be this strong," she admitted, her vulnerability laid bare before him.

"I always believed in that strength," he replied, a warmth blossoming in his chest. "You've faced so much with such grace; it's truly inspiring."

As Maya spoke of her struggles, her laughter broke through the heaviness like sunlight piercing through thick clouds. "Sometimes, it feels like I'm just getting by you know?"

"Life has a way of testing us," Nasser said, admiration swelling within him. "But look at how far you've come."

"Some nights, I'd wake up and miss you so deeply it hurt," she confided, her voice barely above a whisper.
Nasser's heart tightened at her words. "I never stopped thinking about us," he confessed, his voice carrying the weight of his vulnerability.

He shared fragments of his life during her absence—moments that had shaped him, like the books that had opened his mind and the places that had deepened his soul. "Every experience taught me something," he said. "But nothing ever compared to what we had together."

Their laughter bridged the distance between them, soothing old wounds, rekindling a cherished familiarity. They bantered over quirks they still shared, laughter laced with an unspoken truth and forgiveness that neither needed to name.

"There were nights when I missed you so much, it hurt," Maya murmured, her voice barely above a whisper.

Their words formed a fragile bridge across time and pain, their laughter filling in the spaces that days had worn thin. In that honest exchange, forgiveness blossomed like the gentle, silent promise to rebuild the love they'd once shared. The challenges they had faced apart had not broken them but strengthened the foundation for something new.

Nasser's chest tightened, for he'd known that same loneliness, staring at a night sky that seemed to hold its answers just out of reach. "I never stopped thinking about us," he replied, his voice thick with emotion.

As the evening deepened, they spoke not just of the past but of what might lie ahead. A quiet gratitude settled between them for this second chance—a rare opportunity to restore a love that felt as eternal as the stars above.

In life's pivotal moments, choices often arrive like whispers, nudging us to pause and reflect. That night, as Nasser lay awake, thoughts of Maya and of Rashida stirred within him. He realized he wasn't just an observer in his story; he was its author. With that awareness came both the weight of responsibility and the thrilling possibility of change.

Choosing love, he understood, didn't mean abandoning the past; it meant honoring it while embracing the present. It required accepting the full spectrum of human experience, the ache of nostalgia and the thrill of new beginnings. Every step of his journey had shaped him, but love, he felt, was his compass forward.

"Life isn't about waiting for the perfect moment," he whispered to the quiet room. "It's about creating moments in the midst of chaos." The words felt new, though he had always known their truth. "We can choose to find joy amidst uncertainty, to celebrate what we have instead of mourning what we've lost."

Reflecting on the choices that had led him here, the big ones, like leaving for Paris, and the small ones, like picking up the phone, he saw how each stroke on his life's canvas had contributed to a story uniquely his own.

"It's easy to feel life is something that happens to us," he mused softly. "But when we remember we have the power to choose, everything changes."

He saw now that life was made of these daily choices—the choice to open up, to love despite risks, to keep moving toward dreams even as fear tries to hold us back. Each day offered the chance to redefine who he was and who he could become.

As he lay there, a sense of lightness replaced the burdens of the past. Life, he realized, was a journey of choices, each one shaping his path, molding not only who he had been but who he still had the chance to become. He felt whole—a completeness he hadn't known he was missing—born from facing love's complexities without looking away.

And yet, one truth remained clear above all others: his love for Maya had only grown, its absence an ache too profound to ignore. Tomorrow, he decided he would ask her. On their video call, he would look into her eyes and ask the question that had been on his heart all along: "Will you marry me?"

In that quiet, pivotal moment, Nasser understood something with absolute clarity: a life without Maya would be a life without color, without meaning. She was the light that softened his darkest hours, the missing piece that made everything feel whole again. And now, he knew, it was time to fight for the love that had always been theirs.

The morning dawned brightly, carrying the crisp promise of new beginnings. Nasser walked into the café, his heart thrumming with anticipation and a touch of anxiety. As he crossed the street, he saw Rashida seated outside a convenience store, sunlight cascading over her, lending her a warm glow that mirrored the gentle stirrings in his chest.

With a renewed sense of purpose, Nasser bought two espressos, letting the rich aroma ground him. As he approached, the hum of the Parisian streets seemed to fade, leaving only the steady beat of his heart in his ears. Meeting her gaze, he felt as though fate had guided him here, standing at a crossroads between the future he longed for with Maya and the unexpected, soul-stirring bond he shared with Rashida. Life, in its unpredictable wisdom, had offered him love in its varied forms—a love to honor and a future yet unwritten.

"Good morning," Nasser greeted, extending a steaming cup toward her with a warm smile. "Thought you might need a little pick-me-up."

Rashida's face softened in gratitude. "Thank you, Nasser. This is just what I needed."

As they settled into conversation, a familiar ease emerged, as if the noise of the world around them had faded, leaving them alone in an intimate corner of the city. She spoke of her late husband, Khalil, her voice tinged with tenderness and quiet sadness. "He was kind and so full of life," she said, her words thick with nostalgia. "He used to say I was like the sun—always bright, always warm, even when things got hard."

Their conversation ebbed and flowed, light laughter mingling with the rich notes of espresso, each moment offering Nasser a glimpse of her strength. As they spoke, Nasser sensed the sharp, judgmental glances of a few passersby, their gazes a reminder of how easily life's circumstances could change. He pondered how wealth and status could be so fleeting, the sort of things that vanished with the unpredictable turns of fate.

At one point, Rashida reached into her bag, her eyes shadowed with emotion and handed Nasser a carefully preserved letter. "This is the last letter Khalil wrote to me," she whispered. "I read it every day. It's my reminder of everything we shared and everything I had to let go."

Nasser took the letter with reverence, feeling its weight in his hands. He unfolded the paper, his gaze lingering on Khalil's words, each line a quiet tribute to love, loss, and resilience.

Dearest Rashida,

If I seem joyful, it's because I'm remembering our days together, which were nothing short of miraculous. I should feel defeated, but who can truly mourn after knowing such happiness? Have I told you how extraordinary you are? If I haven't, that's a grave oversight.

Facing death while still alive is strange; everyone must eventually face it, yet none of us knows the how or when. I don't fear death itself—what frightens me is leaving you. I can't imagine journeying to another world without you by my side. This is our fate, though, and it breaks my heart to think of you carrying on alone.

It feels as though everything I know is on the verge of being erased, like a storm sweeping away what we thought was unshakable. Life changes without warning, and nothing is guaranteed. Every day may look the same, but it's only an illusion. Change is always present, as constant as the earth's shifting landscapes. Death, too, is inevitable, the final reminder that life does not need our consent to transform. Every soul on this planet is counted, and I believe God is calling me home, with an angel waiting to guide me.

You must trust, Rashida, that life is on your side. You have a strength that will carry you, no matter what lies ahead. Your heart holds a vast reserve of courage, and you'll find it waiting for you when you need it most. Truth and kindness are the twin guides that will see you through any fear and any sorrow. Beneath our fears, our courage shines, stronger than anything we could have imagined. Be gentle with yourself, as we have been with each other, and hold fast to these truths.

This journey has shattered the life we once knew, but it's also shown us the depth of love we are capable of. I feel the ache of incompleteness without you, a longing to shield you from pain. There's so much to fear, and I don't have all the answers. Life's mysteries are boundless, and it takes courage to listen to the voices hidden within our trials. Those voices reveal truths about our path, even when the way forward seems shrouded.

Hold my love close, for it is eternal, transcending both time and space. Let it be your warmth as you forge ahead, a comforting embrace in the journey of life. Remember the laughter we shared, those quiet moments that overflowed with love; they are your armor against despair.

As you navigate a world without me, seek joy in each sunrise, allowing it to remind you of the beauty still present. Surround yourself with kindness, letting it fill the spaces of your heart. Know that you are never truly alone; I will always be with you in spirit, offering gentle encouragement. You carry within you a light that no darkness can extinguish. This is my gift to you, a sustaining presence as you continue on your path.

All my love,
Khalil

As Nasser finished reading, tears pricked at the corners of his eyes. He looked up to find a shimmer of emotion reflected in Rashida's gaze.

Without a word, he draped an arm around her, silently sharing in her quiet sorrow. "It's beautiful," he murmured, handing the letter back to her. "He loved you deeply."

"Khalil taught me that love endures, even when life takes unexpected turns," she replied, her voice trembling slightly. "It's a lesson I will carry with me always."

"Yes," she continued, her voice steady despite the raw emotion in her eyes. "Khalil taught me that love doesn't end; it transforms. It becomes part of us, no matter where we go."

Nasser admired her resilience, wondering how someone could endure such heartache yet remain so open to the world. "You're remarkable, Rashida. You've lived through pain and still find a way to give love freely."

Her smile was a blend of sorrow and warmth. "It's a choice, Nasser. Every day, we can choose to honor those we've lost by living fully in their absence. I learned that from him."

Nasser nodded, contemplating her words. They lingered in the air like a promise—a reminder of love's ability to transcend even the deepest losses. As they continued to talk, he found himself drawn to Rashida in ways he hadn't expected. Her wisdom, grace, and laughter illuminated the shadowy corners of his heart.

"I often felt like a ghost," she admitted, "drifting through Paris in a world that seemed to forget me. It was as if I was constantly searching for something I had lost."

Nasser nodded, his expression understanding. "I think we all feel that way sometimes. It's the human condition—this longing to be seen, to be loved."

"But it's more than that," Rashida continued. "It's the realization that we're all connected by our experiences, our joys, and our sorrows. Each of us carries the weight of our stories, and it shapes who we are."

"Yes," he agreed, his eyes sparkling. "And in sharing those stories, we find solace in knowing we're not alone. It's like a patchwork quilt—each piece unique, yet they come together to create something beautiful."

She smiled at his metaphor, feeling the warmth of his words wrap around her. "That's a lovely way to put it. Life can be messy, but in that mess, we often find the most profound truths."

He couldn't ignore the pull he felt toward Rashida, the way her spirit reminded him of Maya yet remained unique in its own right. There was a tenderness in their connection, a softness that made him feel seen in ways he hadn't anticipated.

"Rashida," he began, hesitating for a moment, "I want you to know that what we share means a lot to me. You've opened my eyes to the beauty in unexpected connections."

Her gaze was steady, her smile inviting. "You're a wonderful person, Nasser. It's rare to find someone who truly listens, who understands the weight of words. I'm grateful for our time together."

The atmosphere shifted, and Nasser felt a warmth pooling in his chest. As they prepared to part, he made a choice in that moment—a choice to keep this connection alive. An exhilarating thrill surged through him. Nasser realized that while Maya held his heart, Rashida had awakened a vibrant part of him. Fear could no longer dictate his choices; he must embrace love in all its forms, with its complexities and contradictions, even if it meant risking his heart once more.

"Rashida," he began, his voice steady and full of conviction, "I want you to know how much your strength means to me. You've shown me that love can bloom even in the darkest of places."

Her eyes widened, and he felt a charge of energy between them—electric and alive.

"You remind me so much of Khalil," Rashida murmured, her gaze searching for something deeper within him. In the warmth of her eyes, he felt his resolve deepen. He knew he would call Maya again, ready to rebuild their love—stronger, with a richer understanding of life's fragility and beauty. Love, no matter the trials it faced, had the power to illuminate even the darkest paths.

15

Togetherness Dawns

Rashida was a woman from war-torn Zarifa who had lost everything but her dignity, resilience, and unwavering courage. For Nasser, this realization was profound, reinforcing his belief that homelessness should never be unfairly associated with laziness. A house reduced to ruins could be rebuilt with determination and strength. Their meeting the next morning was more than just a promise—it was a step toward reclaiming a sense of humanity and dignity for those who had been forgotten. Nasser's heart felt lighter, his path clearer, as he prepared to face the challenges ahead with a newfound sense of purpose and solidarity.

As Nasser passed through the bustling emergency entrance of the hospital, thoughts of Rashida enveloped him like a warm blanket. Suddenly, an urgent announcement echoed through the chaos: "Doctor Hassan to Ward 10, please." The frenetic energy of the hospital buzzed around him, but Nasser's mind lingered on the promise he had made. A renewed commitment—not just to support Rashida through her struggles but to challenge the entrenched prejudices clouding judgment—fueled him. Each patient he encountered, every hurried step he took, was now imbued with this sense of resolve. He remembered that true healing extended beyond the world of medicine; it thrived in empathy, understanding, and unwavering support for those who often remained unseen. Yet, a flicker of doubt nagged at him—could he truly balance his demanding career with his mission to challenge societal prejudices?

The weight of this question pressed on him, but the ember of purpose within him burned brighter.

Nasser's day at the hospital was a whirlwind, each moment contributing to a deeper sense of purpose. He moved from one patient to the next, finding his resolve strengthened with every encounter. He treated wounds, comforted anxious families, and collaborated with colleagues, all while Rashida's story resonated in his mind. As evening fell, exhaustion settled in, yet he felt more connected to his mission than ever before.

After a simple dinner, Nasser initiated a video call with Maya through his trusty computer, his heart both racing and hopeful. "It's truly wonderful to see you," Maya greeted him, her smile radiating warmth through the screen. Nasser mirrored her smile, feeling a flicker of joy amid the day's heaviness. "You too, Maya."

A flurry of emotions swirled within Maya as her heart raced, threatening to spill over in tears. She studied Nasser, noticing the new beard framing his face and the way he appeared noticeably leaner. She longed for the comforting scent of his cologne.

Nasser, overwhelmed by the surge of emotions, felt as if he had finally found his way home. As the soft glow of the screen illuminated Nasser's face, the world around him faded into a blur. His heart raced, a steady drumbeat echoing in his ears as he gazed at Maya's image, her laughter, a melody that filled the room. He could see the light in her eyes, bright and full of warmth.

The weight of the moment hung heavy in the air, and he felt his palms grow warm and clammy with anticipation. He took a deep breath, inhaling the familiar scent of his cologne, knowing this was the moment he had been waiting for.

"Maya," he began, his voice trembling as he leaned closer to the screen. "There's something I need to ask you." The words hung in the air like delicate strands of a spider's web—fragile yet filled with potential. Her smile softened, her brow furrowing with curiosity. "What is it, Nasser?"

He felt the urge to hold her hand, to bridge the distance stretching between them, but instead, he grasped the edge of the table, anchoring himself as his heart pounded with every passing second. "I want to tell you how much you mean to me." As he spoke, he dropped to one knee, the cool floor beneath him a grounding force. The shock in Maya's eyes flickered like candlelight, her mouth falling open in disbelief. Her breath caught, and he could almost hear the silent gasp reverberating through the screen.

"Maya," he said, his voice steadying, filled with earnestness, "you have brought so much joy into my life. Every moment we share, every laugh, every dream… I can't imagine my life without you." Her hand flew to her mouth, and he caught the glimmer of tears pooling in her eyes, reflecting the light like tiny stars. In that moment, the noise of the world around him vanished, leaving only the two of them suspended in a bubble of shared dreams.

"Maya," he continued, his heart swelling, "will you marry me?" The silence that followed felt eternal, the weight of his question hanging in the air. He could see her processing the moment, her lips quivering as a wave of emotion washed over her. Then, a radiant smile broke free, illuminating her face like the sun breaking through the clouds.

"Yes! Yes!" she exclaimed, her voice ringing with joy as tears streamed down her cheeks. A rush of warmth colored her cheeks, and her heart skipped a beat. This was entirely unexpected, yet without hesitation, she exclaimed through joyful tears, "Yes!" In that instant, all doubts evaporated. She knew, without a shadow of a doubt, that Nasser was the man she loved, and she yearned for him to be a permanent part of her life—forever, just as they had once promised beneath the towering tree by the tranquil lake.

Caught in the whirlwind of emotion, Nasser shared his thoughts with Maya: "Daryana is where I belong, where our hearts reside." Eager to unveil another surprise, he added, "Give me a moment; I have something else for you. Please, stay on the call." He reached for his phone, dialing Hassan's number with a mixture of excitement and apprehension. Some things in Daryana never changed, and Nasser cherished that steadfastness. While Maya had already given her consent, he longed for Hassan's blessing.

"Papa, I have Maya on a video call," Nasser announced, his voice bubbling with enthusiasm. "I'm here to seek your blessing to marry her." Hassan's heart soared upon hearing Nasser's voice through the crackling connection. His face lit up with surprise, a wave of overwhelming happiness washing over him. "You have no idea how long I've waited for this moment, Nasser. Of course, you have my blessing!"

"Really? You mean it?" Nasser's relief was palpable. "Absolutely! You've always been like a son to me. Maya deserves the best, and I believe that's you," Hassan replied, emotion thickening his voice. As Hassan looked at Maya beside the glowing screen, words were unnecessary to convey the depth of his feelings. His nod of consent spoke volumes, a silent welcome for Nasser into their family.

With tears glistening in his eyes, Hassan continued, "I just want her to be happy. You'll take care of her, won't you?" "Always."

"Yes," Nasser affirmed, overwhelmed by the gravity of the moment. The poignant pause that followed felt like the world holding its breath. Then, as if a dam burst, Hassan's tears flowed freely, uniting them in a profound, unspoken bond.

As Hassan gazed at Maya and Nasser, a profound sense of contentment enveloped him. Overwhelmed by the happiness that filled the room, his emotions surged uncontrollably. The joy was palpable, filling the air with an electrifying aura of celebration. It mirrored the deep love and unbreakable connection that bound this family together. For Hassan, this was the culmination of cherished hopes and dreams, a realization that his daughter was choosing a life brimming with happiness and love. He couldn't have been happier to be a part of it. For so long, he had harbored a yearning for this very day, a day when Nasser would sincerely seek his blessing to wed his beloved daughter, Maya.

Papa Hassan placed his head in his hands and began to sob. He had always worn his heart on his sleeve, and at this moment, he was unashamedly happy for his daughter. It felt like just yesterday when Maya was a carefree child, reaching for his hand, blissfully unaware of life's complexities. Hassan wouldn't trade his role as a loving father for all the treasures in the world. Yes, it came with sleepless nights and unexpected adventures, but those were the threads that enriched his life, filling him with purpose.

Maya clapped her hands, her laughter slicing through the tension. "I can't believe this is happening! I'm so happy!"

Nasser grinned, the joy bubbling within him. "I'm just as happy. You have no idea how much your father's blessing means to me."

In that precious moment, the bond between father and daughter deepened even further, a connection that would withstand the test of time.

Nadia was upstairs when she heard the air buzzing with excitement. She rushed down to the ecstatic news, her heart pounding with anticipation. She burst into the room, her eyes wide with wonder, and joined in the celebration, her spirit soaring as she embraced the joyful chaos around her.

Nasser could hardly contain his emotions. The echoing distance between Daryana and Paris felt like an insurmountable chasm, a silent reminder of the physical space that separated him from Maya. Every fiber of his being ached to be closer, to hold the woman he loved with all his heart.

He imagined her laughter filling the room, the warmth of her presence beside him, her hand gently resting in his. Miles away, he could still feel the softness of her touch, the way her eyes lit up when she spoke of their future. He yearned to share his days with her, to whisper sweet nothings in her ear, to plan their life together without the barrier of distance.

Nasser knew that their love was strong, resilient, and bound by a promise that transcended the miles between them. Yet, each day spent apart felt like a test of their resolve, a challenge to their commitment. He clung to the hope that soon, very soon, he would close the gap and be reunited with his beloved Maya.

The air around them buzzed with anticipation, their hearts beating in unison despite the space that lay between them. Nasser made a silent vow, a promise that no matter the distance or the challenges they faced, he would always find his way back to Maya, where his heart truly belonged.

The news of Nasser and Maya's engagement sent ripples of excitement through Daryana, igniting a buzz that felt electric. On a beautiful Friday evening, Nadia, Maya's spirited sister, wasted no time in orchestrating a grand celebration. The scene was set for an unforgettable night at Le Jardin d'Étoiles, an upscale French seafood restaurant that had become a cherished gem in the city's culinary landscape.

Le Jardin d'Étoiles welcomed guests with an atmosphere of sophistication and charm. The chic décor invited warmth, adorned with stylish lamps that cast a soft, golden glow, and plush leather booths that offered an oasis of comfort. Low-hanging mirrors reflected the shimmering lights, enhancing the elegant ambiance. For this momentous occasion, a large round table overlooking the tranquil lake had been chosen, promising a spectacular view as the sun dipped below the horizon.

As the evening unfolded, the trio of Hassan, Maya, and Nadia looked absolutely radiant. Hassan, dressed in a sleek black suit, exuded an air of quiet confidence that perfectly complemented the elegance of the evening. Maya, in her stunning black dress, proudly showcased the engagement ring gifted to her by Nura, its sparkle matching the joy in her eyes. Nadia, the epitome of grace, donned a white beaded evening dress that highlighted her timeless beauty, embodying the spirit of celebration. Their laughter and the light in their eyes spoke volumes about the joy this engagement had brought into their lives.

Nasser's parents, eager to partake in this significant moment, made an entrance that felt almost theatrical. Nura, adorned in a breathtaking teal gown, carried a small bouquet of flowers that beautifully amplified the rich color of her attire. These flowers were for Maya. Samir, with his sophisticated charm, looked dashing in a perfectly tailored black suit, bringing an air of dignity to the occasion.

Samir's playful banter with Jacque, the slightly nervous waiter, helped break the ice and set a jovial tone for the evening. As Jacque returned with an uncorked bottle of Dom Pérignon champagne, his smile mirrored the newfound ease in his demeanor as he expertly poured the golden liquid into crystal flutes, the bubbles rising like effervescent dreams.

Once everyone was settled, Nadia, unable to contain her enthusiasm, raised her glass high. "Alright, everyone! Let's make a toast to Maya and Nasser!" Her voice was bright with excitement. "May your love be resilient enough to survive the times yet old-fashioned enough to last forever!"

Maya's laughter rang out, her eyes sparkling with joy. "I love that! I'm so glad you're my sister."

Hassan interjected, "And remember, in this family, we value humor as much as love. You'll need both!"

Samir chuckled, "I'm ready for the challenge. I've heard about the family dinners!"

Nadia teased, "You're in for a wild ride, Samir. We might just roast you during dinner!"

"I welcome it," he replied, raising his glass. "To laughter and love!"

As the glasses clinked together, Hassan beamed, "Our families are united by Nasser and Maya's engagement!"

"Welcome to the family, Maya! You'd better be ready for a lifetime of cherished memories," Nura said, wrapping her arms around Maya in a warm embrace. "I'm so proud of both of you."

Samir leaned in with curiosity, "I have to ask, how did Nasser propose? I want to hear every delightful detail!"

Maya's face lit up as she recounted the moment. "He got down on one knee during our video call and expressed how much I mean to him. He wanted it to be genuine and heartfelt."

Nura smiled, her eyes misting with emotion. "That's so beautiful, Maya. You're going to be an extraordinary wife."

The culinary journey of the evening was expertly guided by Martine, a charismatic young woman with a natural talent for anticipating her guests' desires. As the evening progressed, conversations flowed like wine, rich and inviting. Martine approached the table with an infectious enthusiasm. "What can I get you all tonight? Our oysters are fresh from the coast, and the seafood platter is a culinary delight!"

"Let's indulge in the platter!" Maya exclaimed, her eyes alight with excitement.

"Excellent choice! I'll add the oysters to your order as well," Martine said, jotting down their selections with a bright smile, her passion for service evident.

Hassan turned to Maya, curiosity sparkling in his eyes. "Have you given any thought to what kind of wedding you want?"

"Oh, I have so many ideas!" she replied, leaning in, her voice filled with enthusiasm. "Something intimate, surrounded by close friends and family. Maybe by the lake, where it all feels so peaceful..."

"Count me in for all the planning!" Nadia exclaimed, her energy infectious. "I'll ensure it's the most epic celebration!"

Papa laughed, a deep, warm sound that filled the air. "I'm grateful to have such supportive women in my life!"

As the evening continued to unfold, laughter and the clinking of champagne glasses created a warm, vibrant atmosphere, celebrating well into the early hours of the morning. With hearts full and spirits high, the group decided to continue the festivities at The Blue Note Lounge, a lively jazz and cocktail lounge. The transition was met with cheers, a ripple of excitement coursing through them as they anticipated the night ahead.

The Blue Note Lounge welcomed them with its rich melodies and spirited atmosphere, where the air was thick with music and joy. The family shared stories, dreams, and laughter, each moment drawing them closer together. It was a night to remember, overflowing with love, laughter, and the promise of a beautiful future for Nasser and Maya—a celebration not just of their engagement but of the bonds that would grow stronger with each passing day.

16

Soulful Connections

The following morning, as Nasser made his way through the bustling streets toward the hospital, he felt the weight of anticipation pressing against his chest. The familiar sounds of the city—a cacophony of distant laughter, the hum of traffic, and the occasional bark of a street vendor—filled the air, but all he could focus on was Maya. With a trembling hand, he dialed her number.

"Maya," he began, his voice thick with emotion, "I wish I could have been there for the celebrations last night. I felt this ache of homesickness mingling with happiness I could hardly contain. I'm overjoyed at the thought of spending my life with you, but I miss the joy of our engagement celebration."

On the other end, Maya listened, her heart swelling with a mixture of love and longing. The soft rustle of her sheets accompanied her tender whisper. "Oh, Nasser," she said, her voice wrapping around him like a soft caress, "I wish I could hold you right now. I felt your absence too, but knowing we have a future together makes it all worthwhile."

Nasser's voice softened, infused with warmth. "Your words mean everything to me, Maya. Just hearing your voice brings me closer to home. I can't wait to be with you and build our life together."

Through her tears, Maya smiled, a glimmer of hope lighting up her eyes. "Soon, my love. We'll be together before we know it, and we'll make up for all those missed moments."

Feeling compelled to share, Nasser spoke of a recent encounter with a woman named Rashida from Zarifa. "Maya, a few mornings ago, I met a woman from Zarifa begging on the streets. We started talking, and she opened up about the immense hardships she's been facing."

He paused, allowing the weight of his words to settle in. The clamor of the street seemed to fade as he recalled Rashida's story. "She has no family or support system," he continued, his tone heavy with empathy. "Rashida found herself alone in a foreign country, unable to return home and surviving on the unforgiving streets of Paris. Yet, it's remarkable—her experiences haven't made her bitter. She accepts them with grace. Though some things are beyond her control, she chooses to see her life through a lens of hope and positivity.

Nasser took a breath, his heart heavy with the compassion he felt for her. "Hearing her story has made me profoundly grateful for what we have."

Maya's heart ached at the thought. "Begging? That must be incredibly challenging for her. I've heard the streets of Paris can be merciless."

"Absolutely," Nasser nodded, the sorrow lining his words palpable. "She faces judgment and hardship every day, yet her determination never wavers. I couldn't just walk away," he admitted, the weight of his decision evident. "I invited Rashida to stay with me and gave her some money on your behalf. I even suggested she get a haircut, something you mentioned could lift her spirits."

Maya's voice brightened with admiration. "That's wonderful, Nasser. You have such a kind heart. Rashida is truly fortunate to have crossed your path."

Nasser smiled, a warm sense of fulfillment blossoming within him. "Thank you, Maya. I'm just grateful I could help in some way. It's a powerful reminder of the importance of kindness and connection."

Her voice filled with love and pride, Maya replied, "You're amazing, Nasser. Together, we can make a difference in the lives of those who need it most."

As they ended the call, both felt a renewed sense of purpose and connection, knowing their love and compassion could bring light to even the darkest corners of the world. When Nasser stepped through the hospital doors, he offered Maya a warm goodbye, his voice filled with determination. "I'll call you later," he assured her.

Meanwhile, Rashida made her way to the hairdresser, her thoughts swirling with the many people in need around her. The scent of fresh shampoo wafted through the air, a bittersweet memory of the comforts she had once known. After a simple wash, color, and cut, she resolved to share her belongings with others in the shared house and stocked the cupboards with food for over a week.

As the saffron-colored sky signaled the end of the day, Rashida prepared to meet Nasser. The fragrant herbs from her garden danced in the air as she harvested vegetables for dinner, slipping into a simple yet elegant blue dress that caught the fading sunlight. Leaving a note on the counter, she headed to the butcher and purchased two racks of lamb, their rich aroma filling her senses with anticipation.

When Nasser greeted Rashida on the street, he admired her strength and dignity. That evening, they conversed as if they had known each other forever, the air around them humming with unspoken understanding. Nasser offered to help with dinner, but Rashida gently refused, her warm smile a quiet invitation to connect. As they stood in the kitchen, their bond deepened with each shared moment.

Rashida wanted to share her heart about Zarifa, a place dear to her. "When the armed soldiers arrived by ships and planes, we were bewildered. The sounds of gunfire and the sight of soldiers were foreign to us. We couldn't comprehend why they had come to Zarifa." She paused, letting the weight of her memories settle in the room. "Days turned into weeks, and it felt like their presence only ignited a thirst for vengeance. I can assure you, our people didn't desire war. War is a force of destruction that resolves nothing. Those who dared to resist the soldiers were labeled insurgents and terrorists, their homes reduced to ashes, and innocent people killed in the crossfire."

Nasser listened intently, the gravity of her words hanging in the air.

"This senseless war has been unjust, altering the course of our lives," Rashida continued, her voice steady yet tinged with sorrow. "The relationship between the foreign soldiers and the people of Zarifa was marked by confusion, fear, and powerlessness. The soldiers felt like outsiders, and the purpose of their arrival remained a mystery. The people of Zarifa had no desire for war and quickly realized that the conflict brought nothing but destruction and suffering, with no resolution in sight."

Nasser's heart ached for her, and he quietly set the table for two, the sound of the plates clinking punctuating the silence.

Rashida continued, her eyes reflecting the pain of her past. "Khalil used to say that, at our core, we all share the same desires. We yearn for the safety of our loved ones, dream of discovering new places on holidays, and cherish the warmth of home with our families, far from the shadows of conflict. The world often faces many threats, and wars are justified. Politicians try to create a positive image, showing concern for solving problems and preserving our planet, but it seems there is an underlying addiction to violence among them. They thrive in times of conflict, even as those around them suffer deeply."

Nasser's breath hitched at the weight of her truth, the fragility of peace echoing in his mind.

"The soldiers, once everyday individuals thrust into the chaos of war, grappled with the daunting task of defending ideals, and causes that often eluded their comprehension. Their actions, driven by a complex mix of duty and fear, often descended into disturbing extremes as they fought relentlessly to uphold principles that remained elusive and mysterious. What truly baffled the mind was the stark absence of any exchange of words between the soldiers and civilians, with both sides resolutely convinced of the other's enmity."

Rashida's gaze drifted, lost in thought. "For a time, Khalil and I considered fleeing across the border to Safriz, hoping to find solace there. But a friend's warning shattered that illusion. Even in Safriz, the communities were deeply fractured along religious lines—Jews, Shiites, Christians—entangled in their own conflicts. A simple misinterpretation of sacred texts had driven them apart, and despite the passage of centuries, they still grappled with these age-old divisions. It raises a poignant question: when will humanity find a way to bridge these profound differences? Sadly, it seems we have made little progress."

"Venturing outside became a harrowing experience, as foreign soldiers observed our every move, further deepening the sense of unease and imprisonment," she continued, her voice a quiet reflection to her resilience. "We tried to maintain hope that this occupation would be temporary, but as time passed, it became apparent that the soldiers were not leaving anytime soon."

Nasser, stirring the mint tea, felt the atmosphere shift with each of her words, the kitchen becoming a sanctuary for their shared truths.

"The soldiers themselves, stationed in a foreign land, were also caught in a complex situation. Many of them had little understanding of the culture, language, or the reasons behind their deployment. They were tasked with defending something they could barely comprehend, often leading to actions driven by fear and confusion."

Rashida paused, collecting her thoughts. "In essence, the relationship between the foreign soldiers and the people of Zarifa was characterized by mutual misunderstanding and mistrust. Both sides longed for peace and safety, yet they found themselves trapped in a conflict they neither desired nor fully comprehended. It was a tragic reflection of the broader human struggle to overcome differences and achieve lasting peace."

As Nasser set the table for two, the rich aroma of fresh mint tea filled the room, creating a warm atmosphere that contrasted with the heavy topics they were discussing. Just then, a call from Maya filled the air with anticipation. Nasser's heart raced as he answered, greeted by Maya's melodious voice. Without a moment's hesitation, he felt an overwhelming urge to extend an invitation to Rashida to join their conversation. "Maya, would you like to speak with someone special?" he asked, his excitement palpable.

Rashida eagerly agreed, and the stage was set for a heartwarming union, evident to the connections that can blossom even in the hardest of times.

As Maya's and Rashida's voices intertwined over the phone, a wave of warmth and affection enveloped them, wrapping around them like a soft blanket on a cool evening. It felt as though a magical connection had been kindled, transcending both time and distance. Maya's voice, a harmonious blend of joy and tenderness, resonated deeply within Nasser, filling the room with genuine affection. Yet beneath the surface of this jubilant reunion, a shadow flickered as Rashida felt compelled to share a poignant piece of news.

With a somber pause, she disclosed her intention to return to her hometown, Zarifa, where her dear friend Hana, recently widowed, eagerly awaited her arrival. Rashida's voice trembled slightly as she revealed the heart-wrenching tragedy that had befallen Hana's husband. He had lost his life while delivering essential supplies—an unforeseen twist of fate that caused him to miss the curfew, unleashing a ripple of grief throughout their close-knit community.

The news of this untimely loss sent shockwaves through Zarifa, leaving the community in deep mourning. As Rashida spoke, the laughter faded, replaced by the solemn weight of her words. It was clear that her decision to return was driven by a profound sense of duty to support her grieving friend—a burden pressing against her heart.

Touched by Rashida's dedication, Maya's voice softened, empathy threading through her words. "I can't even begin to imagine what Hana's going through, and I know this must be tough for you. How can we help you during this time?" A moment of silence hung between them, the gravity of their situation settling like the cool night air.

- SOULFUL CONNECTIONS

The warmth of their conversation lingered, an echo of sunlight dipping below the horizon, casting a golden glow over their shared moments. Nasser listened intently, absorbing Rashida's resolve and vulnerability, feeling the weight of her burden settle on his shoulders like an anchor.

"We really need to get ready for what's coming, " Rashida said, her concern evident. Each word resonated deeply within Maya, igniting a sense of urgency and purpose in the quiet room.

"Every generation has faced turbulence and chaos," Rashida continued, her voice filled with determination. "Our ancestors triumphed over challenges with love and purpose. We have to carry their customs and wisdom as we move forward. In Zarifa, you were a friend, a sister, an aunt—always wanted and cherished. Those bonds made us strong enough to face our trials. We have no choice but to accept reality and explore the unwritten life ahead. We have nothing to lose; we need each other. We must unite in Zarifa, focusing on our goals to nurture our relationships with one another and rebuild our lives.

"I love you deeply, dear Maya, even though we haven't met yet. Zarifa is where my roots lie. I can't explain my choice, but it aligns with my purpose in life. I've experienced a life and love that most people only dream of. My life has been a miracle. I hope someday to do something wonderful for you and Nasser." This was no longer just her struggle—it was theirs, a shared journey binding them in solidarity.

In the soft, flickering light of the room, Nasser caught glimpses of Rashida's resilience. He admired how she stood tall, even as she recounted her friend's heartbreaking news. It struck him how powerful their bond was, forged in the fires of adversity.

Maya listened carefully at the other end of the line, her voice a calming presence. "We'll navigate this together," she promised, her tone low but firm, offering reassurance that lingered like a balm in the air. "You don't have to carry this weight alone." Her words underscored their collective strength, a promise to stand united against the shadows that threatened to engulf them.

"Thank you, Maya," Rashida whispered, her voice trembling with emotion. "Knowing you're by my side makes all the difference."

"I believe in us," Maya continued, her voice gaining strength. "If we stand together, we can weather any storm."

Rashida felt the weight of those words settle in her heart like a light of hope. It was a call to action, a reminder that they held the power to make a difference in the face of darkness.

As the conversation drew to a close, Nasser gently reminded Rashida, "Dinner is waiting for you." They exchanged warm goodnights, and Rashida felt lighter, buoyed by the knowledge that Maya was with her in spirit. Nasser promised to call later. The connection between them felt like a lifeline, fortifying their resolve as they faced the uncertain days ahead.

Meanwhile, as Rashida inhaled the rich aroma of roasted lamb wafting from the kitchen, it wrapped around her like the comforting presence of home. As she placed the finishing touches on their meal, her thoughts shifted to Hana and the journey ahead, a mixture of gratitude and sorrow swelling in her chest.

"Thank you, Nasser. The last time I enjoyed dinner like this was with my husband, Khalil."

A soft smile graced her serious expression. Nasser, touched by Rashida's incredible spirit, said tenderly, "Your husband was a wise and caring man." His thoughts drifted to the words in the letter.

"It's a small gesture, but I believe every meal we share strengthens our bonds," she said, a determined spark lighting her eyes. "Tonight, I want to honor our connection."

As they began to eat, Nasser turned his attention to the sumptuous meal before him, savoring each bite with evident delight. He turned to Rashida, a warm smile gracing his lips. "This lamb is perfect, Rashida—tender, succulent, and simply divine. And these vegetables are the best I've ever tasted." The conversation flowed effortlessly, moving through their lives—Nasser's reflections on his childhood, his dreams, and the aspirations he held dear, alongside Rashida's memories of Zarifa, the laughter shared with Hana, and the dreams that once bloomed before the shadows of conflict loomed.

With each shared story, Nasser admired Rashida more. "Hearing you talk about Zarifa brings it to life for me. I can almost feel the warmth of the sun on my skin and hear laughter ringing in the air," he said, pausing to savor the moment. "I wish I could see it through your eyes."

Rashida's gaze softened, nostalgia wrapping around her like a familiar blanket. "It's a beautiful place, full of life, but it's been changed by this war. Yet amidst the turmoil, there's still hope. We hold onto it tightly because it binds us together, even when everything else seems to crumble. I've been like an unopened book on a shelf, unaware of all the suffering in the world. But now, my life has changed in ways I could never have imagined. I can't bring myself to close this book, not even to save my own life. I've never had to worry about anything, not even the weather. I no longer feel the need to rush from place to place. I understand now that my life has taken a different course. It's time for a new chapter to begin, one written with the same strength and confidence that once shaped my life."

Nasser nodded, the weight of her words settling over them. "That's why we must stay connected—to support each other through these dark times. We can't let fear and despair define us." His voice held an urgency that resonated with the gravity of their situation.

As they finished their meal, Nasser rose to wash the dishes, surprising Rashida. "You don't have to do that," she protested, but he waved her off.

"I want to help," he replied, scrubbing a plate with care. "We're in this together, right?"

"Right. Together," Rashida echoed, her heart warmed by his kindness and the comfort of shared burdens.

After cleaning up, they returned to the living room, where the night air grew cooler, carrying the faint sound of crickets chirping outside. Nasser poured them each a cup of mint tea, its soothing fragrance filling the room with warmth. They settled together, the flickering light of a single candle casting soft shadows on the walls, creating a sanctuary of trust.

"Tell me more about Hana," Nasser prompted gently, sensing the heaviness still resting in Rashida's heart.

Rashida took a deep breath, her voice barely above a whisper. "Hana was always the life of our gatherings, full of laughter and kindness. She brought people together, ensuring no one felt alone. Losing her husband has shattered her world, leaving her adrift in a sea of grief."

Nasser listened intently, his empathy palpable. "What can we do to help her?"

"I think she needs to know she's not alone, that her pain is shared. I plan to spend as much time with her as I can when I return—just being there, listening, and helping with practical things like cooking and cleaning." The weight of her commitment hung in the air.

"That's a beautiful way to support her," Nasser said, admiration shining in his eyes. Rashida felt a surge of purpose, her heart swelling with resolve. "Through all of this, I've learned the importance of being there for one another, especially in times of despair. That's how we begin to heal."

"What do you envision for yourself?" Nasser asked, her curiosity piqued.

Rashida continued, "The perception of immense loss can embitter individuals, filling their hearts with anger towards life itself. It takes just one catastrophic event—a hurricane, an earthquake, a fire, or a war—to irrevocably reshape one's existence. The unrestrained hand of fate shows no discrimination; it touches everyone. Fate, with its unpredictable reach, spares no one, tearing down the lives of the privileged and the impoverished alike, altering their realities in ways unimaginable."

Nasser leaned in, his eyes fixed on Rashida's, seeking the essence of her thoughts. "Are you suggesting there's a greater purpose behind these tragedies?"

"No," Rashida shook her head, a solemn expression crossing her face. "I'm not saying there's a divine reason for suffering. But I do believe that in facing these trials, we discover our true strength and resilience. We find ways to support each other, to rebuild, and to create something beautiful out of the ashes. That, to me, is the essence of our shared humanity."

Nasser nodded, captivated by her profound insight. "We have the choice to rise above it, to rebuild and redefine our paths. Like you said, it's about carrying forward the lessons learned, the strength cultivated through hardship."

"Yes," Rashida agreed, her gaze meeting him, igniting a spark of understanding between them. "Together, we can write a new story, one filled with purpose and connection."

As the candle flickered gently, illuminating their shared space, they both recognized the power of their connection—a bond forged in compassion, resilience, and the unwavering promise of hope, even in the face of uncertainty.

17

Rising From The Ashes

It was growing late. Rashida was the first to shower and retire to bed, and Nasser, eager to discuss her, dialed Maya's number.

"So, what do you think of Rashida?" Nasser asked, his tone tinged with curiosity.

Maya's voice was warm and thoughtful. "Rashida's story really inspires me. How does she plan to get back to Zarifa?"

"Maybe she's been saving," Nasser mused. "But we could make it easier for her. I'll buy an air ticket so she can leave on the next flight."

"That sounds wonderful," Maya said, her voice brightening. "I know you've got a busy day tomorrow. With all the flight restrictions, would you like me to help with her bookings?"

"That would be amazing. Thank you. I know Rashida would appreciate it. Her story... it captures something so universal. The way she faces her pain and embraces life's complexities—it's the first step toward healing. She's not allowing bitterness to take root. Instead, she's finding hope amidst the rubble. It's a reminder that even in devastation, there's always a chance for renewal."

Maya paused for a moment before responding. "She is amazing. And we need more of that. There's unrest, Nasser... it's eroding our society. If we let vengeance and hatred fester, they will only feed the roots of violence. We must acknowledge the pain of what we've lost, but we can't let it define us. A city, no matter how shattered, can be rebuilt. Its story can be rewritten."

Nasser listened intently, the weight of her words settling over him. "It's remarkable," he said softly. "No matter how dire the circumstances, people find the courage to rebuild. It's as if there's an unyielding force within us, a will to heal, to mend what's broken. Adversity may knock us down, but it can never extinguish our spirit."

"With compassion in my heart and hope lighting my way, I feel committed to helping Rashida rebuild her life," Maya declared, her conviction clear.

Nasser smiled, touched by her words. "I believe Khalil would be saddened if Rashida allowed her existence to wither into disappointments. Her world was shattered when he passed away. But even in our darkest moments, there's always a path forward. She's been dragged through the streets, humiliated, broken. Yet, she has forgiven—her every fiber craves peace. And it's love that can guide us away from the darkness, toward the light."

Maya's voice softened, her words laced with wisdom. "Nasser, life shapes us in its own way. None of us can escape the transformations it brings. Despite the hurdles, determination and belief will light our path. Life isn't about avoiding suffering; it's about embracing it, learning from it, and rising above it. We must grasp every opportunity life offers. So, make sure you look into those tender eyes each day and remember the extraordinary nature of your own being. The miracles in life are all around us, even in the hardest of times."

Nasser's heart stirred as he absorbed her words. "Thank you, love," he said quietly. "You're right. It's easy to forget the beauty when we're caught in the storm. I'll hold onto that, especially when things feel overwhelming."

"I love you so much, Maya," he added.

"I love you too," she replied. "Let's talk again tomorrow about Rashida's travel arrangements."

They exchanged heartfelt goodnights, and Nasser, after a soothing shower, climbed into bed. But sleep eluded him. Rashida's story had left him with so much to ponder.

Lying in the dark, he recalled the countless moments of suffering he witnessed daily in the hospital. He saw it all—the pain that poured from patients, even as they lay vulnerable and fragile on stretchers. He often overheard their whispered confessions, their pleas for forgiveness, their desperate attempts to make peace with themselves and the world. Even in their agony, they were determined to apologize, to offer love, or to simply find a sense of peace. Pain knew no boundaries, and Nasser realized that through suffering, we are all connected.

Bodies, like all living things, need sunlight, air, and water to thrive. But the soul's needs are different—it craves trust and understanding, for it holds the secret to its true purpose. Hospitals are sanctuaries for the body, but sometimes, people need more than medicine—they need compassion, a healing touch that reaches deep into the heart and soul.

Nasser remembered the words of a gravely ill young man who once confided in him: "I feel compelled to fight. It would be easier to surrender, but my heart would be torn apart if I don't battle this disease." As the young man's condition worsened, the doctors lost hope. He could no longer recognize the faces of his visitors. Yet, in his final days, he had made a choice—a choice to fight. In that decision, he found courage, faith, and an astonishing inner strength. It was a powerful reminder that even in the face of death, we have the ability to choose life.

During one of Nasser's regular visits, the young man whispered, his voice full of love: "Doctor Hassan, please tell your other patients to hold onto their faith and cherish the precious life they have. Sometimes, it takes a tragedy to help us see what truly matters. Suffering opens our eyes to the sacredness of our souls. Cancer humbled me, frightened me, and strangely, it taught me. In the midst of uncertainty, my desire to live burned brightly. I found my self-worth when death came close. I embraced the determination to survive. I was both frightened and brave, stubborn and hopeful. It's as if our will to live resides quietly within us, a light that guides us through even the darkest of times."

Nasser closed his eyes, reflecting on the young man's wisdom. Rashida's journey, too, was one of finding a reason to embrace life, even when it seemed like the world was crumbling. He understood now how daunting it was to navigate a life full of uncertainty, to make decisions that would shape the future. But he also knew that in moments like these, people like Rashida were the ones who proved that life could be rebuilt.

He imagined a future where the children of Zarifa would tell stories of heroes like Rashida—people who triumphed over despair, who rebuilt their lives from the ashes of suffering. They would tell tales of how, amidst the ruins, hope had been born anew. The young hearts of Zarifa would grow up wandering the land like free-spirited clouds, tenderly honoring the wisdom of those who had gone before. They would nurture the fields, knowing the power of renewal, seeing the flowers bloom as symbols of resilience.

Nasser whispered to himself, his voice thick with emotion, "It's a difficult path, but it's the one we must take. People need to move forward."

With those thoughts in mind, Nasser drifted off to sleep, Rashida's journey intertwined with his own, the weight of their shared struggle and hope for renewal heavy in his heart.

As morning light poured into the room, Nasser woke again to the quiet hum of the house. The air was cool, offering respite from the heaviness of his thoughts. He stretched and rose, but when he entered the kitchen, the scent of warm bread and freshly brewed coffee greeted him—a simple, grounding aroma that anchored him in the moment.

Rashida stood by the stove, moving with a calm rhythm. She hummed softly, as though the act of preparing breakfast was a small ritual, a quiet thread of normalcy amid the uncertainty. Nasser lingered in the doorway, watching her.

"Good morning," he said softly, his voice still heavy with the weight of his reflections.

Rashida turned, offering him a gentle smile. "Good morning, Nasser. I thought you might appreciate something simple this morning."

She plated eggs and toast with practiced ease. Nasser sat at the table, watching her. It wasn't just the breakfast that moved him, but the way she carried herself—steady, unbroken, even after everything.

"Thank you," he said sincerely. "You didn't have to do this."

Rashida smiled again, this time a little softer. "It's nothing, really. The least I can do." She set the plate before him and sat across from him. Their eyes met, and for a moment, they shared a silent understanding.

Nasser picked up his fork, knowing that choosing to nourish himself was an act of resilience—a quiet, unwavering yes to life.

18

Homeward Bound

Rashida's face brightened with a gentle, albeit uncertain, smile as she thought about the unexpected free day ahead. "Thank you," she murmured, a hint of hesitation in her voice. The thought of exploring an unfamiliar place on her own was both exciting and intimidating.

Noticing her unease, Nasser wrapped her in a comforting hug. "Don't worry, Rashida," he said softly. "Maya will call later with the travel details. Just take it easy today, let it unfold naturally."

As Nasser headed for the hospital, he flashed a playful grin. "And remember, no sneaking off to any Parisian bakeries today. We need you in top shape for your journey!"

Rashida chuckled. "I promise, no croissant runs today."

Later, the telephone rang, pulling Rashida from her thoughts. Maya's cheerful voice crackled through the receiver. "Hello, Rashida! I couldn't wait to confirm everything for your return to Zarifa."

Rashida smiled at Maya's infectious enthusiasm. "Hello, Maya! It's almost hard to believe. I've missed Zarifa so much."

Maya's joy was palpable. "Your flight is set for 10 p.m. tonight. Nasser's dad, Samir, has arranged everything. A security company will meet you at the airport and take you to Hana's home."

"Thank you, Maya. I'm so touched by everyone's efforts. I've missed home more than I can express."

Despite the warmth of the moment, a quiet sadness lingered in Rashida's chest. She had once imagined returning to Zarifa with Khalil by her side. Traveling alone felt bittersweet.

Maya's voice softened. "I know it's hard without him. But you're so strong, and everyone is eagerly waiting for you."

Rashida's eyes misted over. "I'll do my best to be strong. Thank you, Maya."

Later that afternoon, Nasser received Maya's call with the flight details. His happiness for Rashida was tinged with the sorrow of their impending separation.

When Nasser returned to the apartment, the smell of freshly baked cake filled the air. Rashida had prepared dinner, but the knowledge of her departure cast a shadow over the evening.

Standing before Nasser, her suitcase packed, Rashida's heart ached with the weight of the goodbye.

Nasser, sensing the moment slipping away, asked, "Will you come to my wedding?"

Rashida's eyes softened. "Inshallah! Of course, I will. Nothing could keep me from being there."

The taxi arrived, and Rashida took one last look at Nasser, her heart heavy. "Thank you, Nasser," she whispered, her eyes glistening with tears. After a gentle hug, she climbed into the car, watching him until he faded from sight.

The drive to Charles de Gaulle Airport felt long and lonely, each passing mile deepening the weight of her journey. The city lights faded behind her, replaced by the anonymity of highways and the hum of car wheels on asphalt. As the taxi neared the airport, Rashida turned inward, reflecting on the whirlwind of recent events that had brought her to this moment.

As she entered the airport, the chaos of the terminal buzzed around her, but it felt distant, like she was moving through a world separate from her own. Her steps grew slower as she approached the customs line. The long wait was an opportunity for her thoughts to settle on the journey ahead, but the knot of anxiety in her stomach only tightened.

When her turn came, the customs official's gaze was sharp as he examined her passport. His scrutiny was unwavering, his expression cold. Rashida felt the weight of his gaze like a physical force, each second stretching into an eternity. Her heart began to race.

The official's voice broke through her thoughts. "Madame, do you understand the gravity of overstaying your visa?"

Rashida swallowed hard, fighting the tremor in her voice. "Yes. It wasn't intentional. I got caught up in circumstances beyond my control."

He didn't respond immediately, his eyes scanning her passport with a disapproving air. She could feel her palms sweat, her thoughts scrambling. Would he detain her? Would he impose a fine? Her chest tightened at the thought.

"Circumstances or not, you've violated the terms of your stay," he said, his voice clipped. He raised an eyebrow, waiting for her response.

"I understand, and I'm truly sorry," she managed, her voice barely a whisper. She didn't want to make excuses; she only wanted to be allowed to leave, to move forward.

The official remained silent, tapping his pen on the counter as he pondered her words. His eyes met hers once more. "Do you intend to return to France?"

"No," she said firmly, the answer coming more easily than she expected. The finality of it hung in the air between them.

The official held her gaze for a long moment before stamping her passport with a sharp, resounding thud. "Very well. You are free to go." His tone softened, but only slightly. "Be advised, any future visa applications will be subject to strict review."

Rashida's relief was palpable as she took her passport, her body slackening with the release of tension. She hurried away from the counter, the encounter still echoing in her mind. The knot of anxiety began to loosen, but she couldn't shake the sense that, in some way, she had just left a part of herself behind.

As she made her way to the departure gate, the weight of her return to Zarifa grew heavier. This city, so familiar in its pulse and rhythm, now felt like a place she had barely known. But as she boarded the plane, a strange sense of peace settled over her. She was leaving Paris behind—leaving the uncertainty, the sadness, and the tension. The flight would be a fresh start.

The plane rose smoothly into the sky, and Rashida looked out the window, watching as Paris grew smaller beneath her. The city, with its streets and buildings, now seemed like a distant memory. As she closed her eyes, the hum of the engines became a constant rhythm that soothed her. Each passing mile seemed to lift the burden from her shoulders, and she felt the release, the freedom, of letting go of what was no longer hers to carry.

She let the memories of France fade, not because she wanted to forget, but because they had served their purpose. They had brought her here, to this moment, and now it was time to move forward.

As the hours passed, the soft murmur of passengers and the occasional announcement from the flight attendants became a comforting lull. She sipped her tea slowly, savoring the warmth and the familiar taste. Out the window, she caught glimpses of the world below—vast expanses of land and sea that reminded her of the vastness of her journey, both outward and inward. Each view marked the distance between who she had been and who she was becoming.

When the plane began its descent, the sight of Zarifa's landscape tugged at her heart. A lump formed in her throat as the familiar sights of home came into view, but there was no denying the complexity of emotions within her. This was where her story had begun, where she had both lost and found herself.

The landing was smooth, and as the plane taxied to the gate, Rashida felt her pulse quicken. She was almost home.

She moved through the airport with quiet determination, her steps slow but sure. The once-familiar surroundings now felt foreign, controlled by officials, thick with uncertainty. She knew there were challenges ahead, but the sense of calm she had carried with her on the plane now settled in her chest. It was a quiet strength, a reminder that she was still standing. She was here.

The ride from the airport to Hana's home was long, the vehicle weaving through numerous security checkpoints. The tension in the air was palpable, the soldiers' sharp gazes scanning every inch of their surroundings. At each stop, the guards questioned her, their voices clipped, their eyes hard. Rashida's pulse quickened, but she kept her composure, answering their questions with a calm that surprised even her.

Despite the heaviness of the region's unrest, something within her remained steady. The familiar sights of Zarifa, once colored by memories of pain and loss, now offered a strange sense of peace. This was home, and though the world around her had changed, she had not.

Suliman, her trusted driver, remained silent as they passed through each checkpoint. His presence, though quiet, offered a comfort that she hadn't realized she needed. This was Zarifa, with all its complexities and dangers, but it was still the place where her story began. And it would be where it continued.

The roads were filled with people going about their lives, children playing in the streets, vendors selling their goods, and neighbors chatting on street corners. Amidst the chaos, there was a sense of resilience and community that Rashida found deeply comforting.

As Rashida stepped out of the taxi, the warmth of her friends' smiles was the first thing she noticed. A group had gathered in the yard, their faces etched with joy and relief at her return. Farida, the ever-optimistic neighbor who had been a constant presence in Rashida's life, stood at the forefront. Her arms were outstretched, and her eyes shimmered with unshed tears. "Rashida, you're back!" she exclaimed, her voice breaking as she stepped forward to embrace her. Her warm hug was like a balm to Rashida's weary heart, grounding her in a moment of pure love and familiarity.

Beside Farida was Ahmed, a quiet man with a generous heart who had always been a pillar of strength for Khalil. His deep, steady voice echoed through the yard. "It's good to see you, Rashida," he said, his hand resting gently on her shoulder. The words were simple, but the sincerity behind them conveyed everything she needed to hear—she was not alone.

Across from them stood Rania and her young son, Sami, who had always made sure to bring Rashida small gifts of fresh flowers or fruits from their garden. Sami, with his mischievous grin, looked up at Rashida with a mix of excitement and shyness, holding out a small bouquet of wildflowers he'd picked for her. His gesture made Rashida's heart swell. The children in the group, who had grown so quickly in her absence, ran to her with gleeful abandon. They swarmed around her, their laughter filling the air, offering her the silent strength she had longed for.

Together, they enveloped her in an embrace of collective warmth, their voices rising in unison, each one speaking a language of love, relief, and joy. With every hug, every smile, and every hand that reached out to welcome her back, Rashida felt the weight of her time away melt away. She wasn't just returning to a place; she was coming back to a community that had never truly left her heart. There was no greater gift than that.

Hana, noticing the need for rest and rejuvenation, gently guided Rashida inside. "Come on, you must be exhausted. Let's get you settled in," she said with a soft smile, her arm wrapped protectively around Rashida's shoulders. The air was thick with the sounds of reunion—voices bubbling with excitement, children's laughter spilling into the yard, and the soft murmur of stories being exchanged. This was the life that awaited her. It was imperfect, filled with challenges and heartache, but it was home—the grounding presence of the people she loved and the place that had always been there to hold her when the world seemed too much to bear.

As they reached the doorway, Hana turned back to the gathering crowd. "Why don't we let Rashida freshen up a bit? We'll have time to catch up later." Her voice was warm, inviting, and Rashida could hear the soft murmur of agreement ripple through the group.

Rashida allowed herself to be guided into the house, feeling the weight of the world outside soften as she crossed the threshold. This was the place she could begin to heal, the place where her journey would continue—not defined by the conflict, but by the love and support that awaited her within these walls.

Inside, the house was quiet and comforting, offering her the peace she hadn't realized she so desperately needed. But outside, the hum of voices continued, each conversation laced with care, filling the air with a sense of belonging that Rashida could feel down to her bones. She knew that here, among these people, she would find her footing once more.

Hana led her to a comfortable armchair near the window, the afternoon sunlight casting a gentle glow over the room. "Sit down, I'll make us some tea," she said, her voice tender.

Rashida settled into the chair, the soft cushions offering a welcome respite. She watched as Hana moved about the kitchen, the routine actions filled with a comforting familiarity. It was in these small, everyday moments that Rashida found the peace she had been longing for.

When Hana returned with two steaming cups of tea, they sat together in companionable silence for a few moments, savoring the warmth of the drink and the comfort of each other's presence. Finally, Hana spoke, her voice gentle and filled with concern. "You must tell me everything, but only when you're ready. For now, just know that you are home, and you are safe."

Rashida smiled, feeling a deep sense of gratitude and an aching sadness. "Thank you, Hana. Being here with you, it feels like I can finally breathe again."

As the afternoon light faded into a soft twilight, the two women continued to talk, their voices low and filled with the warmth of shared history and unspoken understanding. They touched on lighter topics at first, but the shadow of recent events lingered.

Hana gently broached the subject, her voice a soft whisper. "Rashida, I'm so sorry about Khalil. I can't imagine how hard it has been."

Rashida's eyes brimmed with tears as she took a shaky breath. "I'm sorry, Hana," she said, her voice catching. "I'm sorry that Ismail was shot just for missing the curfew. I keep replaying that night in my mind, wishing I had been here for you."

Hana reached for Rashida's hand, her grip steady despite the ache in her chest. "It was unfair. It was cruel. But he left this world as a martyr, standing for something greater than himself," she said, her own eyes shining. "And I know—deep in my bones—I know he's watching over us."

She took a breath, willing herself to believe in the strength that had carried them this far. "But you are not alone. We're going to walk through this together."

Because that's what they had learned in the face of so much loss: some things would never be within their power to change. But what they could do—what they *must* do—was hold fast to each other, to the love that still pulsed through their lives, and to the unshakable belief that even in the darkest moments, they could still find a way forward.

Eventually, good things arrive like a gentle spring rain, softening, soothing, tender to your soul. They wash away the residue of past hardships, leaving the air crisp with possibility and the earth fertile with new beginnings. In this moment of grace, you feel the quiet assurance that life is not just about enduring but about embracing these blessings. They nourish your spirit. As the rain nourishes the soil, life invites you to grow, to bloom, and to trust in the beautiful unfolding of your journey.

19

A Distant Light

The ride to Deir Annasia, a small town on the southern border of Zarifa, was steeped in heavy silence, as though the very air held its breath in mourning. Rashida stared out the window, her gaze sweeping over what had once been a vibrant landscape, now reduced to ruins. The buildings, now little more than skeletal remains, echoed the devastation that had swept through the town. Roofs had been blown away, walls had crumbled, and debris littered the streets like scattered remnants of lives once lived.

Nearly a hundred thousand people had been displaced, yet the soldiers still found no evidence of what they had come to uncover.

As Suliman's vehicle jolted through the narrow, crumbling streets, Rashida's heart tightened with each new sight of devastation. Shattered windows, abandoned homes, makeshift shelters—each a stark reminder of the fragility of life in this war-ravaged place. The people who drifted through the streets seemed like shadows, their eyes hollow, their faces etched with a weariness that reached beyond the physical.

"How will we rebuild?" Rashida asked, her voice soft, almost afraid the question would shatter the stillness around her.

Suliman glanced at her, his expression unreadable. He exhaled a long breath, his gaze fixed on the road ahead. "We rebuild for the children who have never known another world," he said quietly. "Yes, Rashida, we will rebuild. We will find a way."

They reached the town square, once the heart of the community, now a haunting ground of loss. Families huddled together, their clothes tattered, their eyes vacant. Children, many of them orphaned, clung to each other for comfort. The innocence in their eyes had been replaced with confusion, pain, and an understanding far beyond their years. The air felt heavy with dust, thick as if the earth itself was holding its breath. The distant hum of murmured conversations and the occasional cough pierced the stillness. Rashida's feet sank into the dirt, grounding her as she stepped forward, heart heavy. The soldiers stood at the edges of the square, their eyes scanning the crowd with cold detachment.

She approached the small group gathered around a fire, their attempts to stay warm contrasting sharply with the cold, impersonal destruction that enveloped them. The adults spoke in hushed tones, their voices carrying the heavy burden of grief and uncertainty. They spoke of loved ones lost, homes destroyed, and futures that seemed distant.

Rashida knelt beside a young woman cradling a child, her arms wrapped protectively around the small form. "We'll find a way back," Rashida assured, her voice soft.

The woman sighed, her eyes heavy with a sorrow. "I don't know... But if we don't try, nothing will be left." She glanced down at the child in her arms, her expression softening. "For them, we have to keep going."

Among them, a young boy sat alone, his knees drawn up to his chest. His eyes, wide and haunted, darted around the square as if looking for something—someone—he could no longer find. Rashida's heart tightened at the sight of him, his innocence shattered in the same way that everything around them had been broken.

She knelt beside him, offering a gentle smile. "Hi there," she said softly, her voice a whisper amidst the murmurs of the crowd. "My name is Rashida. What's yours?"

The boy looked up at her, his face smudged with dirt, his expression guarded. "Ahmad," he whispered, his voice barely audible.

"Ahmad," Rashida repeated, her tone warm and steady. She leaned in slightly, her eyes searching his face. "It's nice to meet you. Are you here with your family?"

Ahmad shook his head, his small body trembling. "They're gone," he murmured, his voice cracking. "The explosions... they took them away."

Rashida's heart broke at the rawness in his voice, and she reached out, her hand resting gently on his shoulder. "I'm so sorry, Ahmad," she whispered, her voice thick with sorrow. "But you're not alone. I'm here for you. We're all here to help each other."

Ahmad's eyes flickered up to hers, and for a brief moment, she saw something flicker in his gaze—uncertainty, perhaps hope. He sniffed, wiping his nose with the back of his hand, then whispered, "Will you stay?"

Rashida nodded, her heart swollen with a quiet promise. "I'll stay, Ahmad. You don't have to face this alone."

They sat together in silence, the crackle of the fire the only sound breaking the stillness. In the distance, the soldiers remained standing, their eyes unblinking and cold, indifferent to the grief that surrounded them. The weight of the world hung heavily in the air, yet in this small moment, Rashida could feel the fragile thread of connection between them.

As the quiet stretched between them, Rashida closed her eyes for a moment, breathing deeply. Gone were the days when the world had seemed filled with possibility, before violence had stolen the light of innocence from so many. Before fear had taken root and taught the world to doubt.

She squeezed Ahmad's shoulder gently, her voice soft but resolute. "I'm so sorry, Ahmad. But we'll get through this together. I promise."

Ahmad's small hand rested on hers, a quiet acknowledgment that her words had found a place in his heart.

Ahmad nodded, his small frame trembling with silent sobs. Rashida sat with him for a while, offering him the quiet comfort of her presence. In that moment, she felt the weight of the world on his small shoulders, and it was impossible to ignore the truth that these children needed more than food and shelter. They needed love, they needed care, and, perhaps most of all, they needed to believe that they still mattered in a world that seemed to have abandoned them.

"I don't know how we can survive this," a woman said, her voice low and weary, as she wrapped her child close to her. "But we do. Somehow, we do."

Rashida smiled gently, her hand resting on the woman's shoulder. "You do. And that's all that matters."

The violence, the destruction—it all made Rashida reflect on the most important things we often lose in the chaos: our voice, our truth, our courage, and our ability to love in the face of cruelty. Violence needs to end for the garden to grow again, for the flowers to bloom. And for that to happen, everyone needs a place where the world quiets enough for the soul to speak.

There is something comforting in stepping back from the world, allowing yourself to sit in the quiet and simply feel whatever you need to feel—without the need to explain it to anyone.

As night began to fall, the dim light from the makeshift tents created long shadows. Rashida joined the team, working tirelessly to distribute food, blankets, and medical supplies. The air was heavy with grief, but there was also a quiet strength among the people—a shared determination to carry on. They came together, offering what little they had, supporting one another in the best ways they could.

Then, an elderly man stood up from the circle and pulled a violin from his side. He began to play. The music, soft and haunting, filled the air, offering a fleeting sense of peace. For a moment, the weight of the world seemed to lift, and the moon, no longer just a distant ball of light, became a guardian of the night. Courage, though fragile, stood brightly in that moment, and the stars above glittered with hope.

Hope. Hope paints in bright colors, Rashida thought, as she allowed herself to believe, if only for a moment, that the world could still be beautiful in its brokenness. The uncertainty of the future faded into the background, and there was magic in the air again.

When the music ended, the old man set his violin down and, with a soft smile, said, "Slowly, piece by piece, we'll find our way back to ourselves—stronger, clearer."

Rashida nodded, her heart full. In a world that often feels unforgiving, it takes extraordinary strength to remain kind, to stay open, and to offer compassion. Even when it's difficult, choosing gentleness is a radical act of self-restraint. It's about refusing to let darkness dictate how we treat others. By responding with kindness, we break the cycle of negativity and create spaces where healing can take root.

This became a nightly tradition. At first, the soldiers tried to break up the gatherings, but Yasin stood his ground. Day after day, he continued, until the soldiers no longer saw a point in interrupting.

Yasin, carrying his violin and his burdens, would say goodnight with quiet grace, standing in the shadow of the moon that seemed to smile down upon them. He had mastered the art of dancing with shadows, of breathing through storms with calm. And every night, he kept moving forward, knowing that standing still was never an option.

As the night deepened, Rashida sat quietly, her thoughts turning inward. She wept for the children whose stained clothes once symbolized a day of carefree play. Today, they had no change of clothes, no softness to shield them from the weight of the world.

In the morning, she would speak to the head of the aid organization, coordinating the safe passage for the women, children, and elderly to Daryana. The soldiers were still present, their cold eyes fixed on every movement, but there was a stirring of hope amidst the tension. She saw it in the small acts of kindness—shared smiles, hands reaching out to help each other.

This fragile hope, though delicate, was a light in the darkness.

Rashida lay down in the tent, her mind restless but determined. Her journey had been long and filled with lonely days, but she knew she was ready to continue. It just happens, she realized, one day—you decide to give yourself another chance. A chance at happiness, at hope, at pursuing the dreams you thought were lost. Even in the midst of despair, there's always room to take another step. Always.

Rashida missed Khalil with a quiet, almost sacred longing, one that filled the spaces between her thoughts like a soft, persistent hum. There were days when the world seemed too sharp, too raw, and she found herself yearning for his presence beside her. She wished, in the deepest corners of her heart, that he had not been called away, that the space between them could have been nothing more than a whisper, rather than this vast, silent space. His absence wasn't just the absence of a person—it was the absence of everything he had been: a light, a touch, a warmth that now echoed in the hollow spaces of her world. She could feel him, though—just beyond her reach, a breath away, in a world she couldn't touch.

She would often find herself standing by the water, watching the sunlight shimmer on its surface, a reflection of a past that no longer existed but still lingered in her heart. "We can whisper and love the way the light shimmers on the water," she would murmur softly, as if speaking to the universe itself, a prayer for the moments she would never share with him again.

For a long time, she had searched for meaning in life, hoping for some grand design to explain the chaos, the heartache, the joy. But now, at last, she understood that there was no meaning to grasp, no grand revelation to uncover. There was only life—this fleeting, fragile thing that could never be contained or controlled. There were no checklists to mark off, no grand purpose to fulfill. There was only the moment at hand, to breathe in, to love, to be kind, to feel. And in that simple, sacred space, she found what she had been seeking all along: the beauty of being fully alive.

In Zarifa, Rashida threw herself into her work, her hands and heart tirelessly devoted to the relief efforts that consumed her every waking moment. The village was in desperate need, and her role there had become both a responsibility and a purpose she could not abandon. Still, her thoughts often wandered—especially to Maya, to the reunion she dreamed of in Daryana. But the urgency of the moment kept her tethered, her plans for the future postponed as she focused on the immediate needs of the people around her. She knew that, in time, Maya would understand. Their bond had always been built on unspoken understanding, a silent promise that no matter how far apart they were, their hearts would remain connected.

The spirit of unity and selflessness shone brightly in Zarifa, much like the light on the water that Rashida often found solace in. This shared purpose created an invisible bond linking personal pain to communal efforts. As Rashida poured her energy into helping others, the community began to thrive under her guidance.

In just six weeks, Suliman's security company successfully relocated thousands of individuals from Deir Annasia to Daryana, most of whom were war victims. Instead of causing discouragement among Daryana's existing residents, this influx ignited a profound sense of community engagement and solidarity. The town's spirit remained unwavering, resolute in the face of significant change. The people of Daryana welcomed the newcomers with open arms, seizing the opportunity to build connections.

One morning, as Rashida prepared to leave for Daryana, she sat with a few of the women she had helped.

"We are thankful for you," one of the women said, her eyes filled with gratitude. "You've shown us what it means to be human again."

Rashida smiled softly, her voice full of quiet conviction. "No thanks are needed. We all have our part to play. We will rebuild, together."

The atmosphere in Daryana buzzed with enthusiasm, making the remarkable transformation hard to miss. Daryana's ethos centered on inclusivity and compassion. Almost every household swung open its doors, especially to the elderly and children among the newcomers. Daryana, once serene, now teemed with vibrant activities, united and thriving, looking after its own.

After a long and arduous year of occupation, a glimmer of hope emerged on the horizon for both the foreign troops stationed in Zarifa and the local population. Rumors whispered through the war-torn streets, hinting that the foreign troops might finally withdraw. This news was like a ray of sunshine breaking through dark clouds, bringing a welcome relief to everyone involved.

The foreign troops had been sent to Zarifa with a sense of duty, but over time, they grew puzzled by their presence in this distant land. They had scoured the rugged terrain, investigated countless leads, and engaged in skirmishes with elusive enemies, yet found nothing substantial to justify their mission. Determination gave way to futility and frustration.

As the possibility of withdrawal loomed, the atmosphere in Zarifa began to shift. The tension that had gripped the streets like a vice slowly eased. People on both sides of the conflict realized they no longer needed to fear each other as adversaries. Cautious optimism emerged, contemplating a future without the heavy presence of foreign troops.

The soldiers grew more familiar with the locals, understanding Zarifan culture and customs, appreciating the warm hospitality despite the circumstances. Bonds formed, transcending language barriers and cultural differences.

The soldiers, far from home for so long, experienced a deep longing for their own countries. They missed their families, the familiar tastes and smells of home, and the simple pleasures they had taken for granted. These feelings of homesickness served as a reminder of their shared humanity with the Zarifan people, who had also endured immense hardships during the occupation.

As the days turned into weeks, the anticipation of the foreign troops' departure hung in the air like a promise of better days. The once-divided city began to heal, and a sense of unity emerged as everyone looked forward to the day the foreign troops would leave Zarifa for good. This anticipation mirrored a broader transition, one that was both collective and deeply personal. The messy middle, that uncertain in-between space, felt ever-present—you're moving on, yet you haven't arrived. You are leaving behind the disruption, but the puzzle pieces are still scattered. There's chaos. There's waiting. There's doubt. You want to rush forward, but progress feels slow. You wait patiently to reach this unknown destination.

This transitional time is for old doors to close and new ones to open. It's a period where things must fall apart so they can come together again. This is a season for being present, for trusting the process. It's a time to pause, to breathe. Have compassion for yourself; you are exactly where you need to be. And though countless days and miles may lie between us and the forces that once held us back, every step we take with the intention to heal is, in itself, a revolution.

Rashida's unexpected arrival in Daryana, accompanied by a group of children from Zarifa, stirred a warmth in Maya's heart that she hadn't felt in years. Their embrace, tender and wordless, spoke volumes—an unshakable bond forged through shared struggles and unwavering care.

As the children settled in, laughing and finding their space, Rashida and Maya retreated to a quiet corner with steaming pots of tea, the comfort of old friendship wrapping around them. Their words flowed easily, laughter filling the spaces between them like a current connecting their hearts.

"I missed you," Rashida's voice was soft, carrying the weight of all that had unfolded. "I'm sorry it took so long to get here."

Maya smiled, squeezing Rashida's hand. "Knowing you, you've probably brought half of Zarifa with you."

Rashida chuckled, the sound lifting the heaviness that clung to the air. "Only half? I must be slipping."

Maya's eyes twinkled, a hint of mischief in her smile. "Seriously, Rashida, you've done more than most could in a lifetime. I understand."

The conversation shifted, the weight of it deepening. Maya leaned in, her expression curious. "So, tell me... what's next for you?"

Rashida met her gaze, the question hanging between them, filled with all the uncertainty and hope of the future. "What's next for all of us? For Daryana? For Zarifa? Some days, it feels like the world presses in on us, heavy and relentless."

Maya held her gaze, the answer coming softly but with conviction. "The world shouts, demands, and pulls—its noise too sharp, its edges too real. And we, caught in the web of its urgency, lose sight of what matters. They say the world's lost its way, but perhaps the truth lies in stepping back, finding solace in stillness, and letting the storm pass on its own. There will be challenges ahead, but there will also be possibilities. And with you by my side, I'm ready to face them all."

In that quiet corner, the future seemed a little less daunting. As they prepared for the next chapter—one of rebuilding, healing, and growth—Rashida and Maya knew that whatever the road ahead held, they would face it side by side, united by a bond stronger than any storm.

A ceasefire deal was now fully in place, and the withdrawal of the troops had begun. The air, once thick with tension, now carried a fragile hope for peace. Families separated by conflict began to reunite, and the streets, once silent and deserted, slowly filled with the sounds of life returning. Though the scars of war would take time to heal, this moment marked a new beginning—a chance for a war-weary nation to rebuild and reclaim its future.

In the soft glow of twilight, there was a gentle promise of renewal. Rashida and Maya stood together, feeling the quiet strength of each other's presence.

As they gazed out at the horizon, a fleeting silence passed between them—an unspoken recognition of all that had been lost and all that had been endured. Maya's voice broke the stillness, soft but thoughtful. "Do you remember what it was like before... before everything changed? How we used to dream of peace, of a world untouched by this endless chaos?"

Rashida nodded, her eyes distant for a moment, reflecting on the years of struggle. "I remember, but sometimes it feels like that person, the one who believed in that peace, is someone I don't quite recognize anymore. We've seen too much. Been through too much."

Maya met her gaze, a slight sorrow in her eyes, but there was also something else—a quiet strength. "I understand. But I think we're both still here because of something more. We're not just the people we were before. We've changed. But in that change, we've found resilience, hope... and maybe even the courage to rebuild what we thought was lost."

Rashida smiled softly, a glimmer of gratitude in her eyes. "I never thought I'd hear those words from you again. But maybe you're right. The world's never quite the same after you've lived through its storms. Still, we have each other, and that's something worth holding on to."

Maya squeezed her hand gently. "We've been through the worst, Rashida. And though we might be different from who we were, we still know what matters. Peace, love, and the courage to keep going."

The journey ahead would not be easy, but with hope in their hearts and love as their guide, they were ready to face it all, hand in hand.

20

Homecoming

At dawn, the world is reborn. As the sun pours its golden light upon the shores, the earth stirs with the quiet intensity of a new beginning. Life awakens, a soft conversation between the wild and the raw, unfiltered. The freedom we find in slumber, unburdened by the weight of our waking thoughts, dissolves as the first rays touch the horizon. And in that light, we rise—stripped of our dreams and fears, yet bound by the insecurities we carry, echoes of all that we are and all that we fear to be.

In the stillness of the morning, listen to the whispers—the quiet stirrings within that speak when all else is silent. Even if you don't fully understand their meaning, heed them. They are the voice of your soul, guiding you toward a path only you can walk. Listen, and let them lead you, gently and unwavering, towards the unfolding of your truth.

With news of the troop withdrawal from Tafara, Nasser felt a powerful pull in his chest: it was time to leave Paris. The City of Light had been his refuge, a sanctuary from the storm, but now his heart ached to return to Maya and the warmth of Daryana. The weight of months spent apart had become unbearable.

There is a subtle difference between allowing someone to hold your hands and chaining your souls together. Listen to that small, persistent voice within, closer than your own heartbeat. The needle of your heart's compass is your truest guide. In the garden of your world, you plant and harvest your own fears, desires, and dreams, moving to the rhythm only you can hear. No one can predict where the wind will take us, but let the soft pearls of snow, falling from heaven's embrace, carry us gently toward where we must go.

With these thoughts, Nasser knew he needed to be there—amidst the changes—reclaiming the life and love he had left behind.

For so long, Nasser had believed that life needed to be understood, that some hidden logic lay beneath the surface. But now, he realized that there was no grand design—only life to live and embrace. There was no singular purpose to chase, only fleeting moments to breathe, to love, to show kindness, and to feel deeply. Life unfolded in the quiet, everyday wonders, often overlooked but always present.

The day of Nasser's return would forever be etched in their hearts. The town hall buzzed with its usual activity when a hush fell over the crowd. Nasser entered, and the room seemed to hold its breath. Maya, engrossed in her work, glanced up. Her eyes widened in disbelief, and her heart soared. She dropped her papers and rushed toward him, arms instinctively opening to welcome him home.

Nasser caught her, pulling her close as if to confirm she was real, that this moment was no dream. Her lips found his in a kiss that lingered, and the world outside seemed to disappear. Tears of relief and joy streamed down Nasser's face, and Maya whispered, her voice trembling with disbelief, "You're really here."

Nasser smiled, wiping away her tears with his thumb. "I'm home, Maya. For good."

As the couple stood there, wrapped in each other's embrace, the months apart seemed to melt away. Around them, the people of Daryana gathered, sharing in this moment of joy. Eyes glistened, and soft murmurs of admiration filled the air. There was a warmth, a peace that Nasser hadn't realized he'd been missing, a profound sense of belonging.

The sun streamed through the windows, casting a golden light that seemed to touch everyone, making them feel part of something beautiful and real. Nura, Nasser's mother, was the next to approach, her hands trembling as they reached out to touch her son's face. She gazed at him with tears in her eyes, murmuring softly, "My boy, you've come back to us."

Nasser pulled her into a tight embrace, his voice thick with emotion. "I missed you, Mama."

Maya and Nura enveloped him in their warmth, the three standing together as a symbol of the resilience of the human spirit—unbroken, united. Nasser felt the bond between them, stronger than ever, and his heart swelled with peace. One day, it just happens. One breath, one moment, one gentle whisper from the universe changes everything. He was home, not just in the physical sense, but in the deepest part of himself.

This reunion marked the beginning of something new—a chapter filled with promise and the strength to rebuild. As the sun began to set over Daryana, casting a golden glow over the town, Nasser knew this was more than a homecoming. It was a new beginning—one filled with hope, love, and the promise of a brighter future.

In the days that followed, Nasser and Maya walked through the familiar streets of Daryana, hand in hand. They paused by the bakery where the sweet smell of freshly baked bread wafted into the air, and

Nasser smiled at the laughter of children playing in the streets. He marveled at how life had continued to bloom despite the scars left by war. It was these simple joys that soothed him, that reminded him of why he had come back.

As the season turned to summer, Nasser and Maya made a heartfelt decision: they would celebrate their love with a lakeside wedding in Daryana. The town, which had longed for a reason to come together in joy, embraced the idea with open arms. Maya had always believed that the most meaningful celebrations weren't built on extravagance, but on love and connection. To gather people together in such a humble yet profound way seemed to shine brighter than any grand gesture could.

For their wedding, Maya knew exactly where it should be—a place that was intimate yet open, where the surrounding beauty mirrored the love they had found. The lakeside gazebo was the perfect choice. Its simple elegance, framed by blooming flowers and climbing ivy, felt like a reflection of their love—steady, quiet, yet strong. It was a place that offered shelter and openness, a perfect symbol of the life they were about to build.

The centerpiece of the evening was a feast fit for royalty. Succulent lamb, slow-cooked to perfection overnight, was presented in all its tender glory, its rich flavor infused with spices. The tender meat was served alongside traditional flatbreads, still warm from the oven, their soft texture a perfect contrast to the crisp, fresh salad greens that added a vibrant touch to the table. The aroma that filled the air was irresistible, drawing everyone in as the scents of roasted herbs, garlic, and smoky meat intertwined with the sweetness of freshly baked bread.

And then there was Valentina, the evening's secret bringer of joy, a woman whose quiet mischief had become legendary in itself. Despite the most careful checks and precautions, she had managed to smuggle barrels of Californian wine all the way from Russia—no small feat, given the obstacles she had to navigate. But Valentina's determination was unmatched, driven by her desire to bring a touch of unexpected joy. The rich, deep red wine, poured generously into glasses, became the evening's unspoken toast. With each sip, the laughter grew louder, and Valentina smiled to herself, knowing that her small but meaningful contribution had added even more magic to an already unforgettable night.

As the guests gathered, the atmosphere was filled with peace. The air carried the soft scent of wildflowers and herbs, and the sun dipped low on the horizon, casting a golden glow over the gathering. It was more than a wedding. It was a celebration of community, of love, and of the healing of a town that had suffered so much.

Whispers of excitement rippled through the crowd as Maya, radiant and timeless, stepped into view. The gown she wore shimmered softly with each step she took, and a delicate tiara of fresh white flowers adorned her hair, adding an ethereal grace. Nasser, the epitome of elegance in his black suit, held her hand with unwavering devotion, his gaze never leaving hers. The crowd watched, enraptured by their love, as they made their way toward the gazebo.

"She looks like an angel," one guest whispered. Another murmured, "They are the most beautiful couple." The crowd's collective excitement filled the air, almost tangible in its warmth. As they reached the gazebo, applause broke out—quiet at first, then growing, a soft wave of appreciation.

Inside the gazebo, Nura, Samir, Hassan, and Nadia stood waiting, their hearts full of anticipation, their smiles reflecting the love and joy that had been restored in Daryana. As Maya and Nasser approached, the world seemed to pause in reverence for the love that had brought them here.

As darkness draped the world, the stars began to appear, one by one, like whispers in the sky. But soon, they were softened by the presence of a full moon, glowing warmly over the lake. Its light seemed to speak to the hearts of those below, reflecting the promise Nasser and Maya had made to each other.

By the water, where they had once shared countless memories, Maya gazed into Nasser's eyes. Her voice was steady, yet full of the love that had grown between them over time. "Nasser, in your arms, I have found a peace I never thought I would know. Your love has been my shelter, my constant, and my protector. I promise to stand by you, as you have always stood by me. Your love is the greatest gift I could ever ask for. Even when the way ahead is uncertain, I will be your calm and your strength, as you have been for me. This is my vow to you, now and always."

Nasser's heart swelled with emotion as he took her hands in his. "Maya, you are my heart, my home, my everything. Through every trial, you have been my light, my source of hope. I vow to honor you, to protect you, and to cherish each moment we share. I promise to always be faithful, to walk beside you, and to support your dreams. With you, I have found my wholeness. With you, I am home."

As their vows were exchanged, surrounded by the quiet beauty of Daryana, the weight of their promises seemed to echo in the air. Each word, spoken from the heart, resonated deeply, forming a bond between them and all who witnessed this sacred moment.

The ceremony culminated in a kiss, a simple yet profound gesture that spoke volumes of their connection. It was a kiss that held the weight of all they had been through, all they had become, and all they would continue to be together. The crowd erupted in applause, and the women celebrated with zaghārīt, their high-pitched ululations filling the air, adding a layer of cultural richness to the evening. Beneath the watchful gaze of the moon, Nasser and Maya stood united, ready to face the future, together.

The stars above twinkled softly, like a thousand tiny promises, while below, the air was filled with laughter and music. People moved freely, their spirits unburdened, caught up in the joy of the moment. It was a night where the world seemed to fade away, leaving only the love and the warmth of shared connection. Children ran joyfully, their laughter blending with the music, while elders shared stories and blessings. Friends embraced, their hearts full of hope and love. The fragrance of the evening feast mingled with the cool night air, grounding everyone in the magic of the night.

As the celebration continued, Nasser and Maya moved beneath the moonlight, their bodies in harmony, the rhythm of the music reflecting the deep rhythm of their hearts. Around them, others danced as well, lost in their own moments of joy and love. It was a night that felt timeless, where the present seemed to hold both the past and the future in its embrace, creating an enduring picture of love and unity.

As the night drew to a close, Nasser and Maya paused for a moment, taking in the beauty of the gathering. The night was not just a celebration of love but a quiet reminder of the warriors who walk among us—those who choose to remain gentle in a world that often demands hardness. It is those warriors of love, like Rashida, whose quiet strength lights the way for others. One day, you decide to give yourself another chance at a life you thought you'd lost long ago. A spark is ignited, a flame rekindled, and suddenly, everything shifts. You rediscover hope, happiness, and a real chance at life.

Rashida's story was one of resilience and dedication, of selfless love that restored what was broken. As she stood quietly amidst the celebration, watching the joy around her, her heart swelled with pride. She saw in Nasser and Maya the love that had brought them all together, and in that love, she found a renewed sense of purpose.

Rashida's journey was one of quiet courage—a reminder that the truest strength lies not in what we overcome, but in how we continue to love, even after the deepest wounds. In a world that often feels cold, she had been the warmth that helped others find their way. And tonight, that warmth was reflected in the unity and joy of the community gathered around her.

Under the moonlit sky, Rashida felt a quiet peace. The love she had worked so hard to cultivate, the bonds she had helped mend, were alive in every laugh, every dance, every embrace. Though her work was far from finished, this night was a realization that we all have the power to love, heal, rebuild, and transform one another.

The night of Nasser and Maya's wedding would be remembered not only as a celebration of their union but as a symbol of the enduring power of love to heal even the deepest scars. In the days that followed, the seeds of hope planted on this magical night began to grow. The community of Daryana thrived, strengthened by the love and unity reaffirmed under the moonlight.

And so, the legacy of Rashida and the warriors of love lived on. Their story was passed down through generations, a revelation that no matter how broken the world may seem, there is always hope. The true richness of life reveals itself when hearts are open to love, and hands reach out to shape the world around us.

The End

www.ingramcontent.com/pod-product-compliance
Lightning Source LLC
Chambersburg PA
CBHW060358080526
44583CB00012B/367